Praise for *Killed to Order*

"A chilling wake-up call that both provokes outrage and poses questions so penetrating and challenging that as a reader you will be moved to ask yourself some very hard questions as you examine your own personal moral code. *Killed to Order* exposes beyond any question and with compelling clarity China's unethical, immoral, and corrupt systemic practice of harvesting 'organs to order.'"

—Phillip "Dr. Phil" McGraw, PhD, clinical psychologist; host and executive producer of the daytime Emmy Award-winning *Dr. Phil* show; bestselling author of *Life Code, Family First, and The Ultimate Weight Solution*

"A lot of what you're about to read I heard directly from Jan, when he first appeared on my podcast to talk about the multi-billion-dollar human organ trade in China. I had no idea that our conversation would go viral, ruffle so many feathers, or lead to this extraordinary book. Spoiler alert: as you read, you will likely experience the same mix of incredulity, horror, and disbelief that I did, when Jan explained to me precisely how and why this atrocity has continued to unfold since 2000. But with every chapter—every page, really—your skepticism will be challenged with some very uncomfortable facts, and you will be confronted with a simple choice: to accept the claims herein as true, or not. Frankly, I wish the evidence was flimsy, or circumstantial, or refutable. I'd prefer to live in a world where human beings are not wrongly imprisoned and routinely harvested for their parts. But I'm afraid that's not the case. The evidence in this book is compelling and credible, and the evidence demands a verdict, no matter how uncomfortable or upsetting the truth might turn out to be. Such are the hazards of pulling one's head from the sand and having a look around at a world in desperate need of improvement."

—Mike Rowe, host of Discovery Channel's *Dirty Jobs*; creator and host of *The Way I Heard It with Mike Rowe*; bestselling author

"As Jan Jekielek shows in *Killed to Order*, when nobody holds perpetrators to account for their escalating 'little atrocities,' they grow in scale and spread to new vulnerable groups. Today's Falun Gong and Uyghurs are yesterday's Jews and Gypsies."

—Robert T. Kiyosaki, bestselling author of *Rich Dad Poor Dad*; Vietnam War Veteran and US Marine Corps helicopter gunship pilot; financial educator and entrepreneur

"If this story seems too unbelievable even for a Hollywood horror movie, it's because this isn't some back-alley black-market isolated crime. This is a state-run system: China's forced organ harvesting industry. . . In *Killed to Order*, *Epoch Times* editor Jan Jekielek courageously lays out the undeniable evidence of China's (CCP) for-profit, Nazi-esque gruesome program of involuntary organ harvesting. Once you know the truth of China's despicable human rights abuses, you can't unknow it."

—Rob Schneider, Emmy-nominated actor and comedian; writer, director, and political commentator

"An amazing exposé of one of the greatest ongoing crimes against humanity and an extraordinarily distilled explanation of the DNA of both generic and Chinese communism. Jekielek shows how the breathtaking atrocity-industry of organs-to-order-by-murder is made possible by a system of perverse incentives that sustain totalitarianism: a system that shapes people whose moral calluses destroy any remnants of human conscience; a system that compels otherwise innocent people to be complicit in crime to achieve survival; a system that rewards the worst, most sociopathic members of society; a system that relies upon lies—all to preserve monopoly control by the Communist Party. It is a system we have refused to acknowledge."

—John Lenczowski, founder, President emeritus, and Chancellor, The Institute of World Politics; former Director of European and Soviet Affairs, National Security Council under President Ronald Reagan

"Actual predators don't announce themselves; they create systems that normalize the unimaginable and abhorrent. In *Killed to Order*, Jan Jekielek reveals that China's forced organ harvesting programs are real—and if one powerful Government does it, others will follow. History offers no exceptions to this rule. We cannot prevent what we deny. Thank you, Jan, for the opportunity to know and resist."

—Gavin de Becker, three-time presidential appointee, bestselling author of *The Gift of Fear*

"This book starts out by focusing on the horrors of organ harvesting, but the real reason this is a must-read is the moral, logical, and political clarity of its critique of the naïve, corrupt bargain lying at the heart of Kissinger's China doctrine."

—Dr. Robert W. Malone, physician and biochemist; pioneer of mRNA technology; bestselling author of *Lies My Gov't Told Me: And the Better Future Coming*

"When I fled North Korea at thirteen, my mother and I crossed into China hoping for safety, only to be captured and sold by traffickers—like so many desperate women, treated as nothing more than property to be bought and used. That horror taught me how regimes and their enablers strip away humanity for gain. Reading Jan Jekielek's *Killed to Order* brought it all rushing back: the Chinese Communist Party's forced organ harvesting turns innocent people into spare parts, murdered on demand. This book exposes that same cold evil, where lives mean nothing against power and profit. We cannot stay silent; we must fight for those still trapped."

—Yeonmi Park, North Korean defector and human rights activist; bestselling author of *In Order to Live: A North Korean Girl's Journey to Freedom*

"This is a chilling and well-documented account, based on survivor testimony and documented evidence, of how the CCP uses the lives of the innocent for both wealth and power. It's a somber reminder that silence enables atrocity, just as it did in WWII. Jekielek's brave and important work serves as a beacon of truth and a call to action to stand firmly against America's greatest enemy. *Killed to Order* is a must-read triumph!"

— Rita Cosby, Emmy Award–winning journalist & bestselling author of *Quiet Hero: Secrets From My Father's Past*

"*Killed to Order* is a gripping, meticulously reported investigation into the systemic human rights abuses at the hands of the Chinese government. It turns a subject most people would find unimaginable into a clear and urgent human story. Jan Jekielek writes with force by clearly laying out the evidence behind their brutality, explaining the machinery behind it, all the while never losing sight of the individuals caught in it. The result is a book that feels illuminating and impossible to shrug off."

—Armstrong Williams, nationally syndicated columnist, host of *The Armstrong Williams Show*, and CEO of Howard Stirk Holdings

"Jan Jekielek documents how China's Communist Party has industrialized evil, ripping organs from the living and committing murder on demand for profit. After reading *Killed to Order*, we can no longer look away from the grotesque crimes of the Chinese regime."

—Gordon G. Chang, bestselling Author of *The Coming Collapse of China* and *Nuclear Showdown: North Korea Takes On the World*; Senior Fellow, Gatestone Institute; columnist, *Newsweek*

"*Killed to Order* is a powerful and compelling story that demands international attention."

—Peter Schweizer, four-time #1 *New York Times* bestselling author of *Red-Handed, Secret Empires, Clinton Cash*, and *Profiles in Corruption*; President, Government Accountability Institute

"With *Killed to Order*, corrupt US political and corporate elites—who have covered for Beijing's crimes against humanity to align the world's oldest democracy with the most vicious regime of our times—have no place left to hide. Nor does China."

—Lee Smith, *New York Times* bestselling author of *The China Matrix: The Epic Story of How Donald Trump Shattered a Deadly Pact*

"The book's telling of profoundly disturbing organ transplantation practices in China is insightful, deeply provocative, and often stunning . . . Jan has managed to spread so much truth and shed so much light on previously obscure areas through his thoughtful and incisive interviews, and he completes that circle of magnanimity with this book that is bound to change any person who reads it."

—Dr. Joseph Ladapo, MD, PhD, author of *Transcend Fear: A Blueprint for Mindful Leadership in Public Health*; Professor of Medicine, University of Florida College of Medicine; former faculty member, UCLA David Geffen School of Medicine; Surgeon General of Florida

"In the shadows of China's authoritarian regime, a vast enterprise systematically harvests organs from living people—political dissidents, religious minorities, and ordinary citizens. In Jan Jekielek's chilling exposé, he uncovers the industrial scale of ongoing organ extraction, revealing a horror that both exposes the moral bankruptcy of China's system of governance and challenges the moral complacency of the reader."

—Jennifer Sey, former elite US national gymnastics team member; bestselling author of *Chalked Up* and *Levis Unbuttoned: My Life in Elite Gymnastics*; former brand President, Levi Strauss & Co.; founder and CEO, XX-XY Athletics

"Jekielek has documented the issue meticulously, without sensationalism, showing why we must confront this adversary head-on. A vital book for anyone who values limits on power."

—David DesRosiers, President, RealClearFoundation; Publisher, RealClear Media Group

"Perhaps the greatest crime of the 21st Century—the industrialized harvesting of organs from political prisoners by the Chinese government—has been largely ignored. In *Killed to Order*, Jan Jekielek exposes, in blood-curdling detail, these atrocities that many would prefer to ignore, and in doing so, reveals why engagement with China was always doomed to fail."

—Chris Chappell, award-winning satirist and commentator; creator, executive producer, and host of *China Uncensored*; contributor, *America Uncovered* and *China Unscripted*

"The mass killing in China of prisoners of conscience for their organs remains an everyday ongoing atrocity. *Killed to Order* confronts us in 2026 with the continuing horror of this victimization and with the criminal regime which perpetrates it. For anyone concerned about human rights or dealing with China, directly or indirectly, this book is a must read."

—David Matas, International Human Rights Lawyer; co-author of *Bloody Harvest: The Killing of Falun Gong for Their Organs*; member of the Order of Canada; 2010 Nobel Peace Prize Nominee

"Jan Jekielek has the courage to fix an unflinching gaze on a crime so ghoulish that most people turn away—namely forced organ harvesting. The nightmares of a hundred dystopian novels have been a reality in China's brutal system of involuntary organ harvesting that turns living human beings into a 'crop' to be exploited for profit. Jan tells this story with a reporter's skill and diligence. *Killed to Order* is a must-read. It leaves the world with no excuse to continue turning a blind eye to this brutal crime."

—Katrina Lantos Swett, President, Lantos Foundation for Human Rights & Justice; Former Chair, US Commission on International Religious Freedom (USCRIF)

"There are two types of China analysts—those that are concerned with their viability within the Chinese Communist Party's China and those that answer a higher calling to speak the truth. In a genuine tour de force, Jan Jekielek plants a spear in the enemy's camp, making a comprehensive case against the Chinese Communist Party and, as a veteran reporter, places the organ harvesting of prisoners of conscience in the center of the indictment—exactly where it belongs."

—Ethan Gutmann, award-winning investigative journalist; author of *The Xinjiang Procedure* and *The Slaughter: Mass Killings, Organ Harvesting, and China's Secret Solution to Its Dissident Problem*; senior research fellow, Victims of Communism Memorial Foundation

"The most difficult topics are the ones about which the least is written. Forced organ harvesting is one of them. It's grueling, cruel, murderous. Everyone knows it is happening and that China and the CCP are the master practitioners. And yet the topic is rarely breached in public. It's nearly a taboo. This silence ends with Jan Jekielek's brave book, *Killed to Order*. It pulls back the curtain and reveals the terror behind the practice. It's a painful but absolutely necessary read that speaks to a core postulate of human rights—the right to life—that seems to be slipping away."

—Jeffrey A. Tucker, Founder and President, Brownstone Institute; *Epoch Times* Senior Economics Columnist; Bestselling Author of *Liberty or Lockdown* and Numerous Works on Economics, Freedom, and Culture; Former Editorial Director, American Institute for Economic Research

"Jan's book is a hallucinatory descent into a Kafkaesque nightmare made real—a 'bad trip' through an Orwellian landscape. Far from being a work of fiction, it serves as a visceral record of horror, a chilling chronicle exposing the full scope of the CCP's cold, systemic logic. It is the ultimate warning of what occurs when an ideological machine replaces human dignity with utilitarian calculus. This is what happens when we ignore sound warnings given by thinkers like Hannah Arendt or Georg Simmel in his *The Tragedy of Culture*. Are we to ignore Jan's warning too?"

—Michel Juneau-Katsuya, former Chief of the Asia-Pacific Bureau, Canadian Security Intelligence Service (CSIS); counterintelligence expert; author of *Nest of Spies* and Co-Author of *Canada Under Siege: How PEI Became a Forward Operating Base for the Chinese Communist Party*

"Just as Solzhenitsyn's *Gulag Archipelago* exposed the Soviet Union's crimes against humanity, so does Jan Jekielek's *Killed to Order* reveal the monstrous deeds of China's rulers. Like Stalin, they rule by terror—arresting, torturing and executing innocents to instill fear in the population. And like other dictators, they have accumulated huge fortunes by enslaving and exploiting the population. . . . Read *Killed to Order*, and then pray that China may one day be free."

—Steven Mosher, President, Population Research Institute; author of *The Devil and Communist China: From Mao Down to Xi*

"It is difficult for anyone in the West to imagine the industrial-scale evil that the Chinese Communist Party has perpetrated against the Chinese people. In *Killed to Order*, Jan Jekielek has done a brilliant job in laying out for the world the sadistic practice of forced organ harvesting within China of members of the Falun Gong and Uyghur communities. It is both a candid and courageous story of what is going on to this very day. Anyone interested in the future of America and Chinese relations must read and understand this important work."

—Brian T. Kennedy, Chairman, Committee on the Present Danger: China; President, American Strategy Group; National Security Expert; author of *Communist China's War on America*

"Too rarely is evil exposed. Jan Jekielek does so in this exceptional book. He reveals the modern face of evil in his careful analysis of the horrific policy of forced organ harvesting in the People's Republic of China. Jekielek demonstrates the true malevolence of the Chinese Communist Party and thus why this monstrous regime must be stopped."

—Bradley A. Thayer, PhD, Fellow, American Freedom Alliance; co-author of *Embracing Communist China: America's Greatest Strategic Failure*

"This book is an education about the threat the CCP poses to our liberty and freedom. It is a must read for all, especially new generations of Americans who have not been informed about this threat and its impact on their future."

—James E. Fanell, career naval intelligence officer whose positions included senior intelligence officer for China at the Office of Naval Intelligence and chief of intelligence for CTF-70, Seventh Fleet, and the US Pacific Fleet (Ret.); co-author of *Embracing Communist China: America's Greatest Strategic Failure*

"*Killed to Order* is a harrowing and meticulously researched exposé of Communist China's systematic, state-sanctioned forced organ harvesting. That such brutality persists in our time is profoundly disturbing. Even more appalling is the silence of world leaders—democratic and authoritarian alike—who choose political expediency and economic interest over moral responsibility. This book is a direct appeal to our shared human conscience, laying out incontrovertible facts and demanding that we confront and end this modern-day atrocity."

—Erping Zhang, President, International Falun Dafa Association; Spokesperson, Falun Dafa Information Center

"*Killed to Order* is a brave and uncompromising book. Exposing state-sponsored killing and global complicity requires rare courage and deep moral clarity—very few dare to do it. Jan writes not from hatred, but from a profound commitment to truth, human dignity, and love of neighbor. This book stands as a necessary testimony and a call to conscience for our time."

—Rosi Orozco, founder and CEO, Kaleido (non-profit organization providing shelters and support for survivors of human trafficking); Former Federal Congresswoman, Mexico; Architect of Mexico's Comprehensive Anti-Trafficking Law

"*Killed to Order* is the book to hand the business executive who talks about how much money there is to be made in China, the politician who talks about engagement with Beijing, the academic who says America is as bad as China. Let them hold this book, and let the blood of the innocent drip through their fingers. From now on, when we see the flag of the Chinese Communist Party, we should know the red represents the blood of the murdered, and those who wave it are bringers of death. . . . If they will do this to their own people, imagine what they will do to people in vassal states. If humanity itself isn't enough of a reason to fight for, survival is. And Mr. Jekielek's book is an essential weapon of truth in the battle."

—Cleo Paskal, non-resident senior fellow, Foundation for Defense of Democracies (FDD); expert on Indo-Pacific geopolitics and Chinese influence operations

"As an Uyghur advocate, I have witnessed the CCP's genocide, brutality, and oppression. Yet this powerful book reveals an even darker reality, the industrialized harvesting of organs from prisoners of conscience, including Falun Gong practitioners, Tibetans, Christians, and increasingly Uyghurs. Jan Jekielek documents how the Chinese state has turned human bodies into a profitable system of exploitation. This is evidence the world needs to confront. *Killed to Order* is a call to action and a warning. No one who reads this book can ever again ignore China's atrocities and crimes against humanity."

—Rushan Abbas, Founder and Executive Director, Campaign for Uyghurs; Prominent Uyghur-American Human Rights Activist

"*Killed to Order* is a rigorously documented examination of one of the most serious human rights abuses of our time: the Chinese Communist Party's systematic use of prisoners of conscience as an organ source. Jan Jekielek brings together investigative reporting, expert analysis, and survivor testimony to reveal how forced organ harvesting operates as a state-enabled industry."

—Fengsuo Zhou, Executive Director, Human Rights in China, Key Student Leader of the 1989 Tiananmen Democracy Movement; Co-Founder, Humanitarian China

"This important book is overdue. . . . While the world has known about this practice in China for over a decade, the overwhelming atrocity of it has caused us to willfully ignore this practice for the sake of maintaining our own sanity. Jan Jekielek is courageous to address this in *Killed to Order*. It is past time that the free world confronts these unspeakable horrors and recognizes the crimes against humanity committed by the CCP. I hope that this book will open a new page in history, where the Western world finally acknowledges these crimes and acts, abandoning business as usual with such a detestable regime."

—Neal P. Dunn, MD, FACS, US Congressman (Florida-02); Chairman, House Subcommittee on Military Personnel; Decorated Former US Army Surgeon and Veteran; Board-Certified Urologist; Lead Sponsor of the Block Organ Transplant Purchases from China Act of 2025 pending legislation

"The Chinese Communist Party is an unrivaled abuser of human rights, driven by a need for totalitarian control and dystopian repression. I am grateful to Jan Jekielek for putting the victims of the CCP first, never forgetting that the Chinese people have always suffered the most at the hands of the CCP."

—John Moolenaar, US Congressman; Chairman, House Select Committee on the Strategic Competition Between the United States and the Chinese Communist Party; Vice Chairman, House Permanent Select Committee on Intelligence

"*Killed to Order* chronicles how the CCP strips and sells the organs of living persons like parts from a car—a grave evil. In it Jekielek illustrates what is at stake in our present struggle for civilization, and the barbarity that awaits us should we lose."

—Larry Arn, President, Hillsdale College; former president, National Association of Scholars; author of *Churchill's Trial: Winston Churchill and the Salvation of Free Governmen*t

"*Killed to Order* is one of the most important books of our time—not simply because of what it exposes, but because of what it demands of us as human beings. Jan Jekielek has performed an act of moral archaeology, excavating a crime so vast, so meticulously hidden, and so normalized by silence that it threatens the very foundations of medicine, ethics, and civilization itself."

—Sayer Ji, Chairman, Global Wellness Forum; Founder, GreenMedInfo and Stand For Health Freedom; bestselling author of *Regenerate*

"Jan Jekielek's compelling book tells a powerful, long-overlooked, and vital story to the world, about the mass murder machine that is the Chinese Communist Party regime."

—Benedict Rogers, Co-Founder and Chief Executive, Hong Kong Watch; East Asia Team Leader, Christian Solidarity Worldwide; Deputy Chair, Conservative Party Human Rights Commission (UK); Author of *The China Nexus: Thirty Years In and Around the Chinese Communist Party's Tyranny*

"Every American needs to read *Killed to Order* for its cogent explanation of Beijing's diabolical policy of forcible organ harvesting—targeting Chinese Falun Gong, Uyghur Muslim, Tibetan Buddhist, and Christian House Church communities . . . This book exposes the utterly amoral character of the increasingly aggressive CCP regime."

—Nina Shea, Senior Fellow, Hudson Institute, and Director of its Center for Religious Freedom

"Jan Jekielek has documented a form of state-sponsored medicalized evil so monstrous and widespread that the mind resists acknowledging its reality. He didn't flinch, however, and neither must we. May his extreme moral courage prove contagious."

—Walter Kirn, bestselling author of *Up in the Air* and *Blood Will Out*; literary critic and essayist; co-host of *America This Week* with Matt Taibbi; former contributing editor, *Harper's Magazine*

"Jan Jekielek's *Killed to Order* is a rigorous, evidence-based exposé that, through survivor testimonies, exposes the CCP's murder-for-profit targeting prisoners of conscience as part of its unrestricted warfare against human dignity and global security. This vital work demands escalated actions—stronger sanctions, scrutiny of transplant tourism, and unified resolve—to confront this evil and protect freedom."

—Dave Harvilicz, Assistant Secretary for Cyber, Infrastructure, Risk & Resilience Policy, US Department of Homeland Security; former Senior Advisor on National Security and Counterterrorism

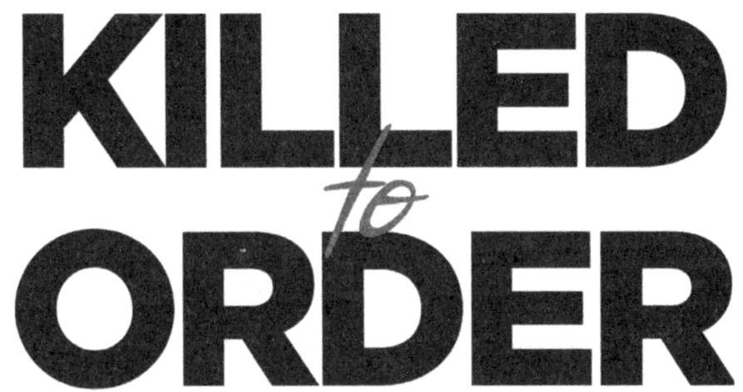

KILLED to ORDER

CHINA'S ORGAN HARVESTING INDUSTRY & THE TRUE NATURE OF AMERICA'S BIGGEST ADVERSARY

JAN JEKIELEK

FOREWORDS BY

AMB. SAM BROWNBACK AND **DR. JOSEPH VARON**

Skyhorse Publishing

Skyhorse Publishing books may be purchased in bulk at special discounts for sales promotion, corporate gifts, fund-raising, or educational purposes. Special editions can also be created to specifications. For details, contact the Special Sales Department, Skyhorse Publishing, 307 Fifth Avenue, 4th Floor, New York, NY 10016 or info@skyhorsepublishing.com.

Visit our website at www.skyhorsepublishing.com.
Please follow our publisher Tony Lyons on Instagram
@tonylyonsisuncertain.

10 9 8 7 6 5 4

Library of Congress Cataloging-in-Publication Data is available on file.

Print ISBN: 978-1-5107-8650-9
Ebook ISBN: 978-1-5107-8651-6

Jacket design by Clay Clark and David Ter-Avanesyan

Printed in the United States of America

For Cindy, without whom this book could never have been written.

"The Party denied the free will of the individual—and at the same time it exacted his willing self-sacrifice. . . . The individual was a multitude of one million divided by one million."

—Arthur Koestler, *Darkness at Noon* (1940)

♦

"And if all others accepted the lie which the Party imposed—if all records told the same tale—then the lie passed into history and became truth."

—George Orwell, *1984* (1949)

"The sad truth is that most evil is done by people who never make up their minds to be good or evil."

—Hannah Arendt, *The Life of the Mind* (1978)

"Let the lie come into the world, let it even triumph. But not through me."

—Aleksandr Solzhenitsyn, *The Gulag Archipelago* (1973)

CONTENTS

FOREWORD
BY AMB. SAM BROWNBACK

I was a young member of the United States Senate over twenty years ago, when I first started hearing these horrific stories of forced organ harvesting on Falun Gong practitioners in China.

I didn't believe them. It just seemed too barbaric, too animalistic. This was something out of the Middle Ages, not the twenty-first century. So I discounted the stories. But they kept coming, one after another.

Eventually, my thinking changed. The Chinese Communist Party has already killed more of its own people than any other regime in history. Why, then, wouldn't it be capable of such barbarism?

I'm sure I was no different than those in the 1940s who doubted the atrocities committed by the Nazis. Until it was too late.

I have toured Auschwitz. I have seen the killing chambers and the shoes and hair collected from the human beings soon to be gassed to death. As well as the pictures of the guards and bookkeepers who looked normal, as if it was just another day at work, not another day of mass murder.

"When we see people no longer as people, but as problems, man is capable of great inhumanity against his fellow man," a wise priest once told me.

Similarly, when the Chinese Communist Party started seeing Falun Gong adherents, and later, Muslim Uyghurs, as problems instead of people . . . horrifying, diabolical disaster followed.

The unthinkable became the Ultimate Utilitarian Solution. If we are going to kill them, let's "harvest" these incredibly valuable organs. We've solved our "problem" and created a highly valuable solution.

Oh what evil the human mind is capable of, and this by "civilized" people!

Jesus would even say, "For out of the heart come evil thoughts and plans . . ."

That doesn't condone it or justify it. It calls us to action to label evil for what it is and cast it out!

Jan Jekielek, in *Killed to Order*, calls evil by name and demands we condemn it with every means we have available.

I do the same in my upcoming book, *China's War on Faith*.

If we do not, our silence is complicity and ultimately, makes us humans capable of accepting dehumanizing solutions to fellow citizens we see as "problems."

Then, instead of "the world changing China. China will change the world," as Lobsang Sangay, the former head of the Tibetan Government in Exile, once prophetically told me.

Read this book and do something! Don't sit on it for years as I did.

We are in an ideological fight to the death with the CCP. The winner will lead the world. A world dominated by Communist ideology is a dark place without room for the spiritual, or for that matter, for Truth, Compassion, and Forbearance, the three guiding core principles of every Falun Gong adherent. Such a world is man as machine, with each of us a disposable cog in a brutalist society.

No wonder the CCP has done everything in their power to

eliminate the Falun Gong from China. *Everything.* This is a clear warning to the rest of us what is coming.

I'm not a Falun Gong practitioner, but there is much to admire in their teachings and practices. I agree with Mother Teresa's sentiment that, "I love all religions, but I am in love with my own." We each are enhanced by learning from one another.

My observation is that of all the religious communities in China, the CCP fears Falun Gong the most, because their approach is the most native to the Chinese soil. It's what Grandmas would practice and teach their families to do in quiet places in their homes, where no listening police could hear.

Historically and culturally, the Chinese people are quite mystically oriented. This is the core of what Falun Gong wants to bring back to Chinese society: a spiritualized culture full of beauty and wonder. It's what Chinese culture was until the Communists came. Communism has no place for spirituality. The CCP views it as its competition for the ultimate authority, which for the CCP must be the state.

We have seen this movie before, even repeatedly, of what happens when government is the ultimate authority over everything.

It is a horror show. We cannot allow our future to go this way!

—Sam Brownback
Co-Chair, International Religious Freedom Summit
Former US Ambassador-at-Large for International Religious Freedom
Former US Senator for Kansas and Governor of Kansas
Author, *China's War on Faith*

FOREWORD BY DR. JOSEPH VARON

MEDICINE WITHOUT CONSENT IS VIOLENCE

I write this foreword not as a journalist, a philosopher, or a theologian—but as a physician. For more than three decades, I have practiced medicine in its most unforgiving environments: emergency departments, intensive care units, and trauma bays where the difference between life and death is often measured in minutes. I have watched organs fail, hearts stop, lungs collapse, and kidneys surrender. I have cared for patients awaiting transplants, and for families clinging to the fragile hope that modern medicine might deliver a second chance at life.

Because of that background, I say this with absolute clarity: What is described in this book is not a medical scandal. It is not an ethical gray zone. It is not a policy failure. It is the weaponization of medicine itself.

Jan Jekielek's *Killed to Order* documents something many physicians instinctively recoil from, often before they can articulate why: a system in which human beings are no longer patients, donors, or even prisoners—but inventories. A system in which organs are not gifts of life but extracted commodities, delivered on demand. A system in which surgery is scheduled not around illness or accident, but around execution.

To those outside medicine, this may sound like a human

rights issue alone. To those inside medicine, it is something far more alarming. It is a warning.

THE ILLUSION OF MEDICAL NEUTRALITY

Physicians are trained—sometimes aggressively so—to believe in neutrality. We are taught that medicine is a technical discipline, separate from politics, ideology, or power. We focus on anatomy, physiology, pharmacology, and outcomes. We reassure ourselves that if the lab values improve and the patient survives, our job is done.

That illusion collapses in the face of forced organ harvesting.

There is no such thing as neutral medicine when consent is absent. There is no such thing as ethical surgery when the donor's death is engineered. There is no such thing as clinical detachment when physicians become instruments of state violence.

What this book exposes, with meticulous documentation, is not simply that organs are being harvested from prisoners of conscience in China—but that the entire medical infrastructure has been reorganized to make this possible. Hospitals, transplant registries, surgeons, anesthesiologists, laboratory systems, logistics chains, and post-operative care pathways all function in synchrony.

This is not rogue behavior. It is systemic. It is institutional. It is intentional. And that is precisely what should terrify the medical profession.

WHY THE WAITING LIST MATTERS

Every transplant physician understands the tyranny of time. In ethical transplant systems, waiting lists stretch for years. Compatibility is uncertain. Organs become available unpredictably, often through tragedy. Surgeons wait—not because they want to—but because they must.

When a system offers guaranteed organs on short notice, with pre-scheduled surgeries and replacement donors standing by, it violates the most fundamental truths of transplant medicine.

Hearts do not become available on demand. Livers are not stocked. Kidneys do not arrive "fresh" unless someone has just died—or been killed.

These are not philosophical observations. They are biological facts.

Jan Jekielek's reporting exposes how those facts are systematically overridden by a regime that has redefined death itself as a logistical variable. In such a system, the donor is no longer a person with rights, history, or family. The donor is a biological match awaiting extraction.

This is not transplantation. It is industrialized killing with a surgical veneer.

THE CORRUPTION OF THE WHITE COAT

The most disturbing aspect of this book is not that a totalitarian regime commits atrocities. History has taught us to expect that. The true horror is that physicians—individuals trained to heal—are placed at the center of the machinery.

Every physician understands what it means to induce anesthesia. Every surgeon understands what happens when circulation is interrupted. Every intensivist understands the precise moment when life ends. There is no plausible deniability here.

To harvest a heart, the donor must be alive moments before removal. To harvest kidneys optimally, perfusion must be controlled. To perform these acts repeatedly requires not ignorance, but participation.

That participation—whether coerced, incentivized, or normalized—represents a moral injury to medicine itself.

When physicians are trained to see human beings as interchangeable biological substrates, medicine ceases to be a healing profession. It becomes a technical arm of power.

TRANSPLANT TOURISM AND SHARED GUILT

Western medicine does not escape this indictment. Patients who travel abroad for "fast transplants" often tell themselves a comforting story: that the organs come from executed criminals, or anonymous donors, or unfortunate accidents. The story is intentionally vague—because clarity would force reckoning.

But ignorance does not absolve responsibility when the warning signs are obvious. When waiting lists disappear, ethics have disappeared with them.

The uncomfortable truth is that transplant tourism creates demand, and demand shapes supply. Without international patients, without Western silence, without pharmaceutical companies supplying immunosuppressive drugs, without academic collaboration and professional normalization, this system could not persist at scale.

This is not an accusation—it is a recognition of interconnectedness.

Medicine is global now. So is its moral responsibility.

A CRIME AGAINST THE CONCEPT OF DEATH

One of the most unsettling insights in this book is how forced organ harvesting distorts the definition of death itself.

In ethical medicine, death is a biological and moral boundary. It is diagnosed, respected, and never manipulated for convenience. In China's organ harvesting system, death becomes fluid—something that can be advanced, delayed, or induced based on demand.

This has implications far beyond transplantation.

If death can be scheduled, then consent becomes meaningless. If life can be terminated for utility, then medicine becomes indistinguishable from execution.

That transformation should concern every clinician, everywhere.

WHY PHYSICIANS MUST READ THIS BOOK

Killed to Order is not merely an exposé of China. It is a case study in how medicine collapses when severed from conscience. It forces physicians to ask questions we are rarely encouraged to confront:

What happens when clinical excellence is decoupled from ethics?

What happens when physicians answer to the state rather than the patient?

What happens when technological capability outpaces moral restraint?

These questions are not theoretical. They are increasingly relevant in a world of algorithmic medicine, bio-surveillance, and centralized health-care power. The lesson here is not confined to one country or one regime.

BEARING WITNESS

Physicians have a unique obligation—not only to treat disease, but to bear witness to suffering caused in the name of medicine. Silence is not neutrality. Silence is permission.

Jan Jekielek has done what many institutions have failed to do: he has documented, named, and refused to look away. This book stands as a record not only of atrocity, but of courage—of whistleblowers, investigators, and survivors who understood that truth must be preserved even when justice is delayed.

For those of us in medicine, this foreword is not an endorsement—it is a summons.

To remember why consent matters.

To remember why waiting matters.

To remember why life cannot be reduced to parts.

Medicine exists to serve the human person—not the state, not ideology, not efficiency, and not power. When it forgets that, it becomes something else entirely. This book ensures that we cannot say we did not know.

MEDICINE AS A MORAL PROFESSION

Medicine has never been merely a technical craft. Long before modern ethics committees, regulatory boards, or international declarations, the physician's role was understood as a moral one. To practice medicine was to enter into a covenant—an asymmetric relationship grounded in trust, vulnerability, and restraint. The patient places their body, and often their life, in the hands of another human being, trusting that power will not be abused.

Forced organ harvesting represents the absolute inversion of that covenant.

Here, the physician no longer stands between the patient and harm, but becomes the mechanism by which harm is delivered. The white coat—once a symbol of protection—becomes camouflage. Surgical skill, anesthetic precision, and logistical coordination are no longer expressions of care, but tools of domination.

This is why the events documented in *Killed to Order* cannot be dismissed as cultural aberrations or political excesses. They strike at the core of what medicine is supposed to be. When physicians participate in systems where consent is irrelevant, where death is instrumentalized, and where human beings are reduced to biologic utility, medicine ceases to function as a healing profession. It becomes a managed process of extraction.

History offers sobering parallels. At various points in the twentieth century, physicians participated in atrocities under the banners of progress, efficiency, and national interest. Each time, the rationalizations were similar: "We did not decide the policy." "We were only performing our assigned role." "The system would continue with or without us." These explanations did not withstand moral scrutiny then, and they do not now.

What makes the modern era uniquely dangerous is the sophistication of the tools involved. Advanced imaging, transplant immunology, surgical robotics, and global supply chains allow atrocities to occur with clinical elegance and administrative distance. Violence no longer appears chaotic or crude; it is scheduled, documented, and billed.

That transformation should unsettle every clinician practicing today.

Because the question raised by this book is not only whether medicine can be corrupted—but how easily. Not through overt cruelty, but through normalization. Not through sadism, but through compartmentalization. Not through hatred, but through obedience and career survival.

Killed to Order forces the reader—especially the medical reader—to confront an uncomfortable truth: that professional identity alone is not a safeguard against moral collapse. Only conscience is.

—Joseph Varon, MD, FACP, FCCP, FCCM, FRSM
President and Chief Medical Officer,
Independent Medical Alliance
Professor, The University of Houston College of Medicine
Houston, Texas

INTRODUCTION

THE "CHINA OPTION"

A DESPERATE SITUATION, A MIRACULOUS SOLUTION

"May" is forty-five years old; she could be someone you know. She could live in Des Moines, Iowa, or the suburbs of Vancouver, or Manhattan, New York. She could be an attorney, or a stay-at-home mother, or perhaps she's a sixth-grade science teacher, a job she loves so much she doesn't even think of it as work. She has a loving husband and two young daughters, eight and ten.

Her symptoms begin subtly—fatigue, swelling in her ankles and feet, a loss of appetite—then steadily grow more alarming: shortness of breath, nausea, muscle cramps, darkening skin, numbness. After months of doctor's visits and a battery of tests, she is finally diagnosed with chronic kidney failure.

Within a couple of years, May's condition progresses to the point that she requires dialysis three times a week, tethered to machines that perform the work her kidneys no longer can. She is suffering terribly—not only from the pain, exhaustion, and relentlessness of dialysis, but from the sense that she has placed an unbearable strain on her family. At times, it feels as though she has abandoned them. She knows they are doing everything they can to hold things together, but their best no longer feels like enough. Their lives are slowly coming apart.

A kidney transplant is possible, but only in the distant future. No one even talks about it. The waiting list is measured in years—often two to five, sometimes longer—so long that it feels almost abstract, and impossible to plan around. For now, there is only more of the same: a slow, painful decline in the quality of May's life, and in the lives of those who love her, and the doctor tells her that less than half of people on dialysis survive to five years. It is enough to make her cry, which she does, quietly, often, and alone.

One day, while waiting for yet another medical appointment, she overhears a conversation between two women. In low voices, they are discussing something they keep calling "the China option." May apologizes for eavesdropping, but asks what they are talking about. "What's the China option?" She would not normally be paying attention, but she's desperate.

The two women exchange a look. They explain: quick transplants, no wait times, organs matched very fast. You might make it. You might get to spend many more years with your family. You might not leave them broken and bereaved. For kidneys, at this point, it's thirty grand.

"Here," one of the women says, pulling out a piece of paper. "It's an ad, but there's some good information. And a broker's name."

When she tells her family about the conversation, they are elated. It seems too good to be true. Is it really possible? Why hadn't anyone mentioned this before? Should they do it? It's a lot of money, but it's for the family, for the future. Who can put a price on health?

"It seems risky," May tells her husband.

"What do we have to lose?" he asks. "If it works, just think . . . "

She doesn't have to think. All she's been able to *do* is think: What happens if it works? It would be . . . a miracle.

"Let's do it," she says.

May calls the number on the ad, speaks to a broker, and they agree to the terms. Though it all seems legitimate and too good to be true, May does not ask too many questions. She is surviving at this point more on hope than anything else. When the money is paid, no receipt is given, only a note that, for all intents and purposes, says nothing.

The broker arranges everything. Blood samples are sent ahead. Within days, a match is made, and travel arrangements are set. May will fly to China, and the surgery will take place at the Shanghai Number One People's Hospital. It's a stark building, far from the bustling street. There is a transplant ward with thirteen rooms, three beds each. Patients come from Singapore, Taiwan, the Philippines, Japan, Hawaii—all over the world.

When she arrives, everything goes according to plan. May is picked up from the airport and travels, in relative comfort, to the facility, where she meets with doctors and nurses. Nothing about it seems remotely suspect, and any concerns she'd been harboring begin to fade.

The operation will be tomorrow at dawn. May is isolated in a sterile pre-op area. She does have one question, though, which she asks one of the doctors: Who is the kidney coming from? She feels grateful to the donor.

All she is told is that the kidney will be sourced fresh. She doesn't ask any more questions.

Before the operation, cross-matching is done, and the kidney, when it is delivered, is found to be incompatible. The organ can't be used. It happens, they explain, but not to worry, there are more donors. The next day, another kidney is brought, and this one is a match. The operation lasts about four hours. Four other patients receive their kidneys the same day. May sees them around as she recovers.

For the next five days, she remains in the hospital under observation. Then another seven in an ordinary room. After about two weeks, May returns home with two souvenirs: her new kidney, which is functioning perfectly, and a small booklet containing information about aftercare. That's it.

For a while, she's constantly reminded of her new kidney, and of the whole strange experience. There's the recovery, first, and the pain. But then there's just a scar, which itself fades. In time, she puts the whole experience behind her. She moves on with her life, profoundly grateful to have it.

But one day she reads a news report that catches her eye. It tells of a woman, a whistleblower, claiming that her surgeon husband has performed thousands of surgeries on Chinese prisoners without their consent. She suddenly feels a sharp pain, a pang of awareness. She remembers something someone told her—maybe the broker, maybe a doctor—that the organs came from death-row prisoners. But that's not what the whistleblower says. She says the organs came from political and religious prisoners, people who practice something called Falun Gong, a spiritual practice persecuted by the Chinese Communist Party with hundreds of thousands of practitioners locked up.

May's hands are shaking as she reads on, a terrible thought dawning on her: that someone died—no, that a person was murdered—so that she could live. A wave of nausea hits her. She feels disgusting, violated, guilty, complicit, criminal. She thinks of calling the broker, of demanding answers, but she knows what he will say. And anyway, she's alive, isn't she? *These things are complicated,* he'd told her early on, when she'd asked for a few more details. *What matters is the end result: you get to live. For a long, long time.*

Yes, she thinks now, but at what cost?

A CONVENIENT TARGET

May's discovery, which was enough to make her sick, is actually just the tip of the iceberg.

Whistleblowers first sounded the alarm over systematic forced organ harvesting in 2006. One of them, a medical staff member in a northeastern Chinese hospital, told *The Epoch Times* that her neurosurgeon ex-husband removed corneas from detained Falun Gong practitioners and that the remains went straight to the incinerator for cremation.[1] An independent people's tribunal, chaired by war crimes prosecutor Sir Geoffrey Nice KC, confirmed in 2019 that forced organ harvesting had been occurring across China under the state's watch, with Falun Gong practitioners "used as a source, probably the principal source of organs."[2]

Falun Gong makes a convenient target. The spiritual practice, which drew about 70 million to 100 million people by the late 1990s, has been targeted by the regime since 1999. Its practitioners meditate daily, don't smoke or drink, and aspire to a peaceful mindset—healthy lifestyle habits that researchers suggest have made their organs ideal for the organ transplant trade.[3]

To avoid implicating their friends and families, many Falun Gong practitioners refuse to give their names when police officers detain them. And without official records, they are easy prey for the illicit organ trade, where secrecy is key. "There has been a population of donors accessible to hospitals in the [People's Republic of China] whose organs could be extracted according to demand for them," the Tribunal said in its Judgment.[4] Chinese authorities, it states, "would have no difficulty in committing Falun Gong practitioners to any fate," turning them into a ready donor pool.

One former Chinese official connected to organ harvesting, the overseer of the health department of the Chinese army logistics branch, told undercover investigators in 2014 that taking organs from Falun Gong practitioners was an order from the top.[5]

A PROJECT TO COMBAT DEATH

Why? An elite obsession with longevity, survival, and rejuvenation.

Chinese officials have eyed replacing organs as an option for rejuvenating life since the late 1970s, when China's organ transplant industry was in its infancy. In 1978, according to a US-based Chinese-language magazine, now known as the *China News Digest*, medical workers harvested kidneys from a political prisoner right after execution. The organs went to the child of a high-ranking official who was suffering from kidney failure.

As the practice proliferated underground, regime leaders kept a tight lid on the health records of the political elite. Nonetheless, accounts of organ transplant surgeries on political dignitaries have trickled out over the years.

In 2023, the death of former Chinese Deputy Cultural Minister Gao Zhanxiang made headlines after an obituary inadvertently divulged that he had replaced "many organs." The eighty-seven-year-old had changed so many body parts that he once joked that "many components are not his own anymore," the obituary read.[6]

The historical lineage of projects aimed at boosting health and longevity dates back even further, almost to the Party's founding. As early as the late 1920s, while struggling to survive civil war in China, the fledgling Chinese communists already had a hospital for treating their top leadership. Not long after the communist party assumed control over China in 1949, the communist authorities began a 100-acre farm staffed with soldiers to supply fresh dairy and produce for officials near Jade Spring Hill, according to a Chinese state history magazine. The area, commonly known as the "back garden" of Chinese politics, is home to private villas of high-ranking military leaders.

The farm, the magazine article said, cultivated rare off-season foods that first Party chief Mao Zedong enjoyed, such as seedless watermelon, which didn't become commercially available until at least the late 1990s.

Between the 1960s and 1970s, injecting blood from young soldiers was a popular "tonic" for senior communist officials, Li Zhisui, Mao's personal physician for twenty-two years, wrote in his 1994 memoir, which was published in the United States and banned in China.[7]

Whatever the latest fad in the hunt for longevity, one theme remained constant throughout the years: the ruling elite has always come first.

Chinese communist cadres get free premier health care in VIP patient wards; for those at the top, a select panel of nutrition experts deliberates on what they should eat, Chinese media reports show.

In 2006, Chinese state media quoted a former deputy Chinese health minister as saying that four-fifths of Chinese health-care dollars serve the 85 million Chinese Communist Party members. The official later walked back the statement after a nationwide backlash. It's unclear if it was truth, or simply bluster.

"Protecting the leadership," when it comes to health, is a national priority, a deeply-placed China source once told me.

Dr. Ning Xiaowei, a cardiologist who worked in VIP wards at a major Chinese hospital, recalled that a deputy provincial official summoned specialists from the best hospitals across the entire province to treat an injury.

Ning said it was a textbook case of how the Chinese communist hierarchy works.

"The so-called people's servants have the entire Chinese population serving them," she told *The Epoch Times*.

The special treatment for the elites shows in the data.

In the late 1970s, when Chinese people lived to sixty-eight years on average, the top communist statesmen reached their late seventies and eighties, an *Epoch Times* analysis of public data found.[8]

One of the longest-living people in China's modern history was Zhang Lixiong, a major general of the People's Liberation Army. He died in April 2024 at the age of 110. Former State Councilor Song Ping, who is still alive, is 108.

THE HOT MIC

The once-obscure and deeply secretive forced organ harvesting industry came into the public eye in 2025 after a hot mic moment between the Chinese and Russian leaders, who discussed the prospect of longevity via multiple organ transplants and made reference to a 150-year life span. Chinese state television captured the hot mic musings on Sept. 3, 2025 as Chinese leader Xi Jinping escorted his Russian and North Korean counterparts to an enormous military parade at Tiananmen Square in Beijing. "Earlier, people rarely lived to seventy, but these days at seventy you are still a child," Xi told Russian President Vladimir Putin, prompting the latter, who, like Xi, is seventy-two, to reference continued organ transplants as a key to immortality. "Predictions are that in this century, there's a chance of living to 150," Xi said just before the audio faded.

That longevity claim harks back to a one-minute ad in 2019 promoting the 301 Hospital in Beijing, China's top military medical center dedicated to treating those in the top political circles.

"A 150-year lifespan project to combat death," the voiceover in the ad calls it.[9]

The clip describes a health system decades in the making, combining the best of traditional Chinese medicine with Western technology. At one point, the voiceover touts the system for the Chinese elite as "tried and true" and first-rate, backing up the claim with a graph that depicts Chinese leaders outliving their American and British peers by at least a decade.

The bold declaration troubles medical ethicists.

"Sickness is not something that is turned on and off like a light switch," Dr. Torsten Trey, executive director of Doctors Against Forced Organ Harvesting, told *The Epoch Times*. "It is one thing to talk about staying in power and becoming 150 years old. But how would they do that?"[10]

A CRIME AGAINST HUMANITY

There are still many unanswered questions about China's forced organ harvesting industry—questions with grave implications for the future of medicine, the future of morality, and the future of the free world.

But thanks to the tireless work of investigators, reporters, and unbelievably courageous Chinese whistleblowers, we know far more than we did two decades ago. We know for certain that Falun Gong, Uyghurs, and other groups are still being targeted. We know that the Chinese Communist Party will stop at nothing to ensure its own survival. And we know that Western elites and Western media are being steadily co-opted, and made complicit in the CCP's crimes against humanity.

At the end of the day, that is what forced organ harvesting is, a crime against humanity, and we must not allow ourselves to forget the human element.

At the exact same time that May is making her way to China, traveling to the airport, flying across the ocean, sitting in the back of a car, and lying down in an operating theater in Shanghai, a dark, deeply evil inverse journey is taking place: the donor's.

We know almost nothing about the prisoner—not even her name—because she will not survive her part of the story.

Perhaps she had been arrested months earlier for protesting the government's treatment of Falun Gong. Perhaps someone asked whether she was a Falun Gong practitioner, and because one of Falun Gong's core tenets is truthfulness, she answered yes. Perhaps someone threw a picture of Li Hongzhi, the founder of Falun Gong, on the ground and said, "Step on it," and she refused. Many of the people around her, it seems, have been poisoned into believing Falun Gong is something it is not—something dangerous and evil. She has witnessed a massive propaganda campaign—something like half a million distinct pieces published when the persecution began—to dehumanize her and her fellow practitioners, many of whom had been pillars of their communities and pictures of health.

Perhaps she went to the police herself and argued that Falun Gong practitioners are good people, and that they should not be harmed.

In any case, she was arrested and thrown into a prison camp.

In prison, she was tortured, abused, and treated with relentless cruelty. A range of instruments was used—electric batons and other sadistic contraptions. It was a living hell. She saw people disappear. She heard screams in the distance. She screamed herself. But she was also subjected to extensive medical testing—blood and tissue tests, and organ scans, far more sophisticated and expensive than anything she had ever seen before.

It made no sense. *Why treat me as subhuman and then spend so much time checking my health?* she would wonder.

She began to hear whispers and threats from the guards: reform or else. *Or else what?* she thought. *They are already torturing me. I'm barely a human in this place.*

Then one day, she is taken from the prison to the very same hospital in Shanghai. No explanation is given. The journey is shorter, rougher, and far less comfortable than May's. In the hospital, everything is perfunctory, mechanical. She barely has time to think, even as the answers to her earlier questions—why the tests? What did the guard mean by "or else?"—come into focus.

Perhaps she is told she's there for more tests. Perhaps no one says anything at all. She is quickly prepped, opened, and harvested. There is no reason to let her live to tell the story, no matter how implausible it might sound. So it is agreed, as it always is, that she cannot wake up. And she doesn't. Ever.

Her death is ruled a suicide, as it so often is with Falun Gong practitioners, despite the fact that Falun Gong explicitly forbids self-harm.

Perhaps someone in the hospital, a nurse, or even a doctor, pauses over her lifeless body and looks upon with something like sadness, guilt, or shame. But perhaps not. There is no time. There are many more surgeries to perform that day, and the next, and the next.

PART I

A NEW FORM OF EVIL

CHAPTER 1

A RUMOR SO EXTREME IT'S HARD TO BELIEVE

ANNIE

In 2006, the ex-wife of a Chinese surgeon in Northeast China—alias "Annie"—went to the press with a ghastly, shocking testimony. Her story was almost impossible to believe.[1]

Almost.

"I found out about this at the end of 2003," she said. "At the time, my husband had become absent-minded and almost robotic. He had been doing it for years but had never told me about it. He often had terrible nightmares and would wake up shrieking and terrified. He would stare blankly at the TV. When our child or I touched him, he would shriek. I found him becoming abnormal.

"He told me, 'You have no idea of my agony. These Falun Gong practitioners were alive. It would be okay if we removed organs from dead bodies, but these people were truly alive.'"

She claimed he carried a mobile phone with him at all times, and any time it rang, day or night, he would immediately go to remove organs from Falun Gong practitioners, who were still alive at the time of extraction.

A group of surgeons, Annie said, worked together to remove all major organs, even the skin, and the dead bodies were cremated. Between 2001 and 2003, about three thousand to four thousand Falun Gong practitioners died as a result of forced organ harvesting at the hospital she and her husband worked at in Sujiatun, according to estimates by some of the doctors involved.

By the time Annie went public, she estimated that her husband had personally forcibly removed the corneas from about two thousand Falun Gong prisoners of conscience.

In separate interviews with *The Epoch Times* and David Kilgour, a former MP and prosecutor in Canada, Annie told the rest of her story:

"My ex-husband and I worked at the Liaoning Provincial Thrombosis Hospital in Sujiatun between 1999 and 2004. My ex-husband used to be a neurosurgeon who participated in removing organs from Falun Gong practitioners.

"Our hospital started to detain these Falun Gong practitioners in 2001, about 5,000 to 6,000 of them. Live organ removal was conducted secretly. At that time, I did not know about it.

"This hospital removed organs from a large number of living Falun Gong practitioners. Some practitioners were still breathing after their organs were removed against their will, but they were thrown into the hospital's incinerator anyway. The hospital's incinerator in the boiler room was also used as a crematory oven.

"At the beginning, fearing information could leak out, different organs were removed by different doctors in different rooms. Later on, when they got money and they were no longer afraid, they started to remove the organs together.

"If the victim's skin was not peeled off and only internal organs were removed, the openings of the bodies would be sealed and an agent would sign the paperwork. The bodies would be sent to the crematorium near the Sujiatun area. If the skin was removed, they would be sent to the hospital boiler room.

"[My ex-husband] was asked to help out [with organ removal] in other hospitals. Every time he did this, he got lots of money and cash awards—several dozen times his normal salary . . . hundreds of thousands of US dollars.

"The majority of the Falun Gong practitioners were transferred from Dabei Prison, Masanjia Forced Labour Camp, and other prisons in Shenyang. Others were kidnapped from parks or their homes. They were kidnapped because they refused to give up their belief in Falun Gong. The police didn't have any search warrant, and their families didn't know it when they were arrested. Because the Chinese communist government's state policy authorizes killing Falun Gong practitioners without any legal consequences, the death of Falun Gong practitioners in China's penal system is nothing. So far, no Falun Gong practitioner has come out alive."

The hospital where Annie and her ex-husband had worked only handled the removal, and the organs were sent to other hospitals throughout China.

"This whole scheme and the trading of organs was organized by the government health system. The doctors' responsibility was simply to do what they were told to do," Annie said. "These things were done in secret. The surgeons involved in our hospital were actually interns transferred from other hospitals."

Because the lives of Falun Gong practitioners are not protected by the Chinese Communist Party, the intern doctors were instructed to use Falun Gong bodies for experimentation.

"There were a lot of transfers in and out of our hospital. Some doctors felt very pained after they had done it. Some were transferred elsewhere. Some changed their names and moved elsewhere. Some went abroad. Some may have been killed to eliminate evidence.

"Other people know about it but do not dare to speak up, as they are afraid of being killed.

"In 2004, I asked my husband to quit his job and he agreed. However, quitting put him in mortal danger. . . . We received threats by phone at home, and we were the target of an assassination incident. . . . My family decided to run away from everything by moving abroad.

"I have divorced my husband because I cannot accept the fact that he removed organs from Falun Gong practitioners. I myself have been severely traumatized and devastated.

"This is a state crime. I know this is the state that is committing the crimes. I know I alone will not be able to change this, but I know a lot of doctors will step out. I truly hope that these doctors, after hearing my heartfelt testimony, will act according to their conscience."[2]

I have to admit that when I first heard Annie's story, I didn't want to believe it. I had, at that point, been involved for several years with trying to save the lives of Chinese Falun Gong practitioners, who had been living under extreme state persecution in China since 1999, and rumors and whispers of forcible organ harvesting from prisoners in China had been circulating among different dissident groups for a while. But I'd never taken these stories entirely seriously, hoping they were simply exaggerations, perhaps even just rumors among long-suffering Chinese dissidents hoping to draw antipathy to the regime.

I justified my skepticism in several ways. For one thing, there was never any "smoking gun" evidence, just insinuation. For another, details were scarce—who was doing the surgeries, where, on who exactly? It was frustratingly difficult to pin down anything concrete.

But the real problem, if I'm being completely honest, was that the kinds of horrors Annie described are not easily absorbed by a rational mind. In retrospect, I'm reminded of Jan Karski, the Polish resistance courier who risked his life to bring eyewitness accounts of the Holocaust to the West, only to find that no one could believe him. The atrocities he described—to anyone who would listen, including US Supreme Court Justice Felix Frankfurter and, later, President Franklin D. Roosevelt himself—were so far beyond imagination that even sympathetic listeners dismissed them. They were impossible, beyond the realm of human capability. Of course, Karski's reports turned out to be true, and I shudder to think that, had the right people believed him before it was too late, an untold number of lives could have been saved. But such trust requires an enormous amount of moral imagination—an ability to grasp evil on a scale that defies reason. But even that's not enough. One needs the courage to believe what the mind rejects.

With Annie, my reaction was revulsion. I simply couldn't accept that her story could possibly be real. It sounded too fantastical, too implausible, too evil, even though I knew that the Chinese Communist Party was in charge and I had a visceral understanding of how bad communist systems could be. (My parents had literally fled one when they left Poland for Canada in the 1970s.) But the depths of China's totalitarian machine of repression weren't yet clear to me. That understanding would come later, little by little, over the next two decades.

At that moment, I simply didn't get it. Not yet.

Nevertheless, reporters at several outlets, including *The Epoch Times,* which I had recently started contributing to, along with a number of independent experts, found her account credible. So, I resolved to keep my eye on the story and see how it unfolded, but from a distance.

In my heart, however, despite my doubts, something about Annie stayed with me—an intuition I couldn't quite shake, a sense that there was more to it than I was willing to believe.

The truth will come out, I thought. It always does.

DR. LAVEE

It would not take long.

As it happened, concurrently, in Israel, another shocking story alleging a large-scale Chinese organ-harvesting operation had surfaced. It was just as implausible, but it, too, carried that same unsettling and undeniable hint of truth. This situation involved an Israeli cardiothoracic surgeon named Jacob Lavee. Dr. Lavee, who had once served as head of the Israeli Transplant Association, was widely regarded as a pioneer—a hero, even—in the transplant surgery community. Especially in Israel, where the small population size makes transplants a particular challenge.

A little before Annie's story came to light, Dr. Lavee had made a shocking discovery himself. He was treating a patient in desperate need of a heart. The prognosis was grim. Eventually, the patient essentially told him, "Look, I'm tired of waiting. I'm going to China to get the heart I need in two weeks. They've already scheduled it."[3]

Dr. Lavee was incredulous, but the patient didn't seem to mind. He flew to China, received a heart transplant, and returned home. There were some complications, but the end result was undeniable: the patient got a heart and lived. At first, Dr. Lavee couldn't make sense of it. A scheduled heart transplant? On a two-week timeline? There was no medical scenario in which that's ethically possible, he thought. A heart can only be transplanted from a donor who has just died, and that donor has to have died *very* recently. The only way to know in advance when someone is going to die is . . .

Dr. Lavee couldn't believe it, but it had happened, nonetheless. That was the moment he realized something horrifying was transpiring. He had heard about Israelis going to China for kidney transplants for years, but being a heart transplant surgeon he had never dug into it, assuming people were selling those organs.

"Not that it's okay, not that it's proper, absolutely not, but the idea that somebody will die for the organ never crossed my mind," he told me.

The experience propelled him to devote himself to reforming Israel's transplant laws, a mission that would occupy him for years. Dr. Lavee would go on to become one of the most outspoken and respected advocates in the early movement to expose and end forced organ harvesting. The legislation he championed barred Israel's national health-care system from covering transplants performed in China.[4] It also introduced a reciprocity principle: anyone eligible to receive an organ had to be willing to donate one. This reform increased the domestic supply of organs and strengthened Israel's transplant system.

Still, in the beginning, he was fighting an uphill battle in bringing attention to this topic.

People simply couldn't believe it. Or they didn't want to. I know I didn't. But at a point, when the evidence and the stories became too much to ignore, it was no longer an abstract political issue; instead, it had become deeply personal.

A PERSONAL CONNECTION

My journey into the world of Falun Gong had started several years earlier, in 2000, while searching for a way to heal from an illness that had all but derailed my career.

By the late 1990s, my background and education in evolutionary biology had led me to the study of lemurs. Part of my research involved frequent travel to Madagascar, where I worked at several field sites. After one of those trips, in 1998, I came home feeling unwell. Over the course of about a year, I began losing sensation in parts of my body. My hands no longer responded with precision, and I struggled to do fine work. I was bone-tired and depressed—burnout wasn't uncommon for doctoral students in biology, but this felt like something deeper.

Eventually, I checked myself into the University hospital and doctors discovered that I had a parasitic worm infection, which, compounded by mono, exhaustion, and other health issues (in my own assessment), had triggered Guillain-Barré syndrome—an autoimmune condition in which the body attacks the peripheral nerves of the nervous system. At the time, there really wasn't a way to treat it, and there is no known cure. Many people recover, but some are left with lingering weakness, numbness, and pain. I seemed to be one of the unlucky ones. My symptoms persisted.

I was based in Alberta, Canada, at the time, working in my lab and traveling regularly to field sites. The work demanded fine motor skills, physical strength, and stamina, and it became clear that my health had taken a serious toll. I had to rethink everything—what I could do, what I wanted to do, and whether I'd even have the capacity to continue in science. The illness, which effectively put a stop to my lab work, had taken a major toll on my research, and the many partnerships I had developed to facilitate my work around the world evaporated. It did more than make me sick, exhausted, and depressed; it killed my degree and my career.

Feeling frustrated and failed by mainstream medicine, I began exploring alternative approaches. One of them was something called Falun Gong, which I'd heard about from a friend who had suffered from chronic fatigue syndrome. The friend, whom I knew from a local coffee shop near the University of Alberta, gave me a VCD (a sort of low-resolution DVD) to watch. It was all about the practice of Falun Gong and included instructions on a series of qigong exercises—movements—and meditation. To be clear, I wasn't expecting it to work, but I was open to the idea. And I was, frankly, a bit desperate.

So, I started practicing, doing my best to understand what the teacher on the video was explaining. Surprisingly quickly, I began to feel the sensation of energy somehow coming back into my body. Encouraged, I continued. The exercises reminded me of the slow-motion Tai Chi exercises I had briefly done for relaxation purposes while in high school.

The only problem was, I knew I wasn't doing them quite right. So, to try to perfect the exercises, I visited with the local Falun Gong group at the University of Alberta. There, I was introduced to the main text of Falun Gong, "Zhuan Falun," which explained that the core Falun Gong principles were Truthfulness, Compassion, and Tolerance, and that *that* was what I was really practicing. The exercises were, in a way, supplemental. At that time, I didn't digest much of what was in the book, but I kept an open mind, and I kept practicing.

The strangest part was that, for reasons I couldn't explain at first, my Falun Gong practice seemed to work. And as I practiced, my body began to heal. I saw my neurologist for a scheduled visit some months after having started, and she stunned me. "You are in complete remission," she said. "Whatever it is you're doing, keep doing it!" I was elated, but as a scientist, I also wanted to understand why it had worked. I was trained to approach everything through the lens of evidence and mechanism, and this practice in my mind lay far outside that framework. Still, I couldn't deny what I experienced.

I didn't fully understand it, but it worked.

Soon, the mother of one of the local Falun Gong practitioners who was a postdoctoral researcher at the University of Alberta arrived in Edmonton and told me her story, a story I would hear many times over the next few years: how Falun Gong practitioners were vilified and persecuted in China and how she had been tortured as a result of her practice. As she was telling me all this—with her daughter translating—it was as if a bolt of lightning went through me.

As I said, I had known since my early childhood that

Communism was bad. But I never really understood exactly *why*, and I'd always puzzled over some of the strange "post-communist" habits my parents seemed to have. Like the way they would react to the idea of my mentioning any family issues outside of the household. To them, it was an act of near-treason.

As the woman spoke to me, I had a deep, instant realization: *this* is Communism at work. The Chinese Communist Party had singled out Falun Gong practitioners for persecution precisely because they viewed them as a threat to the Party's control over the individual—the ultimate goal in any communist system. I suddenly understood many of the things that my parents had tried to instill in me, but that I had rejected, either out of ignorance or perhaps a lack of context. My next thought was: I have to help these people. The more I looked into it, the more I understood that a massive injustice was being perpetrated against Falun Gong practitioners, people who were trying their utmost to be kind and decent and good. More than that, they were innocent, nothing like the "heretical religion" slander the Communist Party was trying to convince the Chinese population, and later the world, of.

I wasn't sure yet how I could help, but knowing what Falun Gong had done for my own life, and understanding the suffering they faced in China, I felt I had no choice but to try.

The stars first aligned when I got a job running international youth exchange programs, where I met my wife, Cindy—a Jewish woman of Polish extraction whose father had survived the Holocaust, and who was, luckily, as fascinated by me as by my commitment to challenging crimes against humanity. The two of us fell in love; I now had a life partner, and quite literally to this very day, a much better half.

Fortunately for me, the stars would align once again. In 2004, Cindy and I started working with the Falun Gong Human Rights Working Group, which would partner with UN-accredited

NGO's to try to make an impact in stopping human rights violations at the UN Human Rights Commission. It was possible to work with UN "special mechanisms," such as the Special Rapporteur on Torture, who at the time was an Austrian human rights lawyer named Manfred Nowak. We would "translate" detailed cases from Minghui.org, the secure website where details of Falun Gong practitioners who were being persecuted were published as general information but also for the benefit of activists, into "UN-speak," which were then assessed for veracity by the Special Rapporteur's team.

When a case was deemed credible (and with our legwork, they always were), Nowak would send it to the Chinese mission, which would then have twenty-four hours to respond to the allegation. The Chinese would always deny there was any issue as a matter of course, but it still proved effective in saving lives. The Chinese officials *knew* that the UN officials had detailed knowledge of harm being done to a Falun Gong practitioner, and in many cases, they would ease the pressure of the persecution on them (though also in several cases, prisoners were still tortured to death).

In the end, however, we were able to help save a few lives. We even traveled to Geneva for the Commission meetings in 2005, where we discovered that despite the hard work of some heroic staff of free countries and nonprofits, the majority of the attendees were there primarily to subvert the process. A dispiriting realization to say the least, but an important one. It was good to find out just what we were up against.

And right as we were contemplating this, another opportunity opened up.

It so happened that as a part of my other work running youth programs focused on community development and education, my wife Cindy and I were sent to Thailand. I went out into the countryside for my projects; Cindy, for the time being, settled in

Bangkok. Cindy had worked in Thailand before and had developed a remarkable grasp of Thai language.

In Bangkok, Cindy discovered what was essentially an underground railroad helping Falun Gong practitioners escape China. They came through the Golden Triangle—the notorious jungle borderlands where Thailand, Laos, and Myanmar collide in a chaotic tangle of drug smugglers, human traffickers, and armed militias—and if they were lucky, they made it to Bangkok, where an office of the UN High Commissioner for Refugees allowed them, at least in theory, to apply for and receive refugee status.[5]

But the situation between Thailand and China was complicated. And one of Cindy's early realizations was that, because of the delicate political relationship between the two countries, Falun Gong refugees were in real danger of being sent back to China. Thailand has never signed the Refugee Convention, and refugee protection there exists only at the discretion of the government. Most refugees keep a low profile. But Falun Gong practitioners—whom I would describe as extraordinarily courageous, though others might use the word "overzealous"—were anything but quiet.

While most refugees were content to hide out, Falun Gong practitioners would gather in front of the Chinese Embassy holding large signs that read "Stop the killing" and "Stop the persecution." The Thai authorities would, in effect, play both sides. They often tolerated the protests, but occasionally, to appease the Chinese, the police would warn the protesters that if they showed up the next day, they'd be arrested.

Inevitably, some would show up anyway. True to their word, the police would arrest them and soon schedule their deportation to China unless they could obtain refugee status in one of the roughly six asylum countries available at the time—the United States, Canada, Australia, New Zealand, Sweden (along with Norway and the other Nordic countries to a small extent), and Germany. Cindy and I found ourselves using our privileges as Canadians to stop Falun Gong refugees from being deported back to China. Unexpectedly, we could access spaces and speak to officials in ways even some high-ranking Thais couldn't. In every case that we attempted, we were able to help facilitate asylum on behalf of those detainees.

At the time, that felt like the best and most meaningful use of our skills.

I wanted to tell these people's stories. Ian Johnson, a reporter for the *Wall Street Journal,* had written a Pulitzer Prize–winning expose of the CCP's persecution of Falun Gong in 2001, which was very powerful and inspiring, and I wanted to follow in that tradition.[6] I approached a number of mainstream media companies, and was incredulous that they seemed uninterested. That's when I came across still-fledgling *The Epoch Times.*

The Epoch Times was the only outlet then willing to report honestly on Communist China. We—the West—had been captured by a big, false, grand narrative that if America pumped enough cash into Communist China, it would liberalize and eventually become a South Korea or a Taiwan. We would change them, have them become more like us. But having recently started working to help Falun Gong practitioners overcome the persecution from the Chinese regime, I knew this was a pipe dream. Above all, these refugees had incredible stories to tell, documenting what was happening to them both inside China and beyond its borders. The Falun Gong practitioners' uncanny resilience to their persecution against all odds was a remarkable, often harrowing story, and no one else seemed willing to touch it.

So, under a pseudonym, I began writing articles about the persecution of Falun Gong, drawing from the people I met in Thailand.

Knowing what I knew, after Annie's revelations and after what Dr. Lavee revealed, I was left with very little doubt: the organ-harvesting claims were true.

In early 2006, when I happened to be on at trip to Poland, I was contacted by Sen Nieh, a professor of engineering at Catholic University in Washington, DC, and also a China human rights activist, explaining that ten thousand people in Israel had signed a petition to expose it. A panel was to convene at the site of the Auschwitz concentration camp to expose the evidence of China's organ harvesting program. As a native Polish speaker, they asked if I could help set it up, which, of course, I did.

I ended up reporting on it as well, for *The Epoch Times*. "There is compelling evidence of widespread illegal organ harvesting in China, said a panel of human rights advocates from the United States, Israel, Australia, and Poland, at *The Epoch Times*-sponsored 'Never Again: Appeal to the World' Forum in Auschwitz, Poland on May 9," I wrote. "Panelists, speaking at the Auschwitz Center for Dialogue and Prayer, also called for an urgent independent international inquiry into the allegations, to stop a possible accelerated slaughter of camp inmates in advance of a new Chinese law restricting organ harvesting from prisoners."[7]

The article went on:

> "The numbers just don't add up," said Dr. Jianmei Yu, Project Leader of Pre-Clinical Research Collaboration at the US Iomai Corporation. An "unexplained" organ bank is the only way to account for a large disparity between Beijing's published numbers of executions, and the orders of magnitude-larger numbers of transplants advertised by organ transplant centers in China.
>
> Chinese Deputy Minister of Health Huang Jiefu admitted in November 2005 that 95 percent of organ transplants in China come from executed death row prisoners.[8] However, in just one of the over 400 hospitals performing organ transplants in China, Tianjin Orient Organ Transplant Center, more organ transplants are performed

than could reasonably come from the sum of all executions across China, said Dr. Jianmei.

After initial allegations of an organ harvesting death camp in Sujiatun, Shenyang Province surfaced in March of 2006, the Chinese communist regime waited for three weeks before denying the charges. Then, on the following day, it announced a new law that would restrict future organ harvesting from prisoners. Chinese insiders have suggested that the law could be a message to those involved in illegal organ harvesting to close up shop, because of increased international attention.

The two sources exposing Sujiatun have said that the organs were taken almost exclusively from incarcerated Falun Gong practitioners. Panelist Ms. Zhizhen Dai, whose husband was captured, tortured, and killed by Chinese authorities in 2001 because he practiced Falun Gong, urged the world to act to stop the torture and slaughter of innocent people.

Journalists calling various organ transplant centers around China in late March and early April discovered many hospitals were urging prospective patients to come in as quickly as possible for their transplants, as fewer organs would be available in the near future. This led investigators to fear the worst: That people are being slaughtered for their organs at an accelerated pace before the new rules come into effect.

Israeli panelists brought with them a petition signed by over 10,000 Israelis urging the discussion of Chinese organ harvesting death camps specifically in Auschwitz.

They included Larisa Vilsker, whose father was one of two members of her Polish Jewish family who survived the holocaust.

"My whole existence and consciousness would not accept or believe that this phenomenon can still happen," she said, speaking about learning of the recent evidence of organ harvesting in China.

"Hundreds of thousands of people are submitted to harvesting their internal organs for sale. I see it as my moral obligation to call, with your assistance, to the international community, to expose the heart of such evil quickly."

A GROWING BODY OF EVIDENCE

Between Annie's story, the work of Dr. Lavee, and the courage of others who had started to come forward, a body of evidence pointing to unspeakable crimes against humanity was beginning to take shape. But it wasn't until David Kilgour, a former Canadian MP and Secretary of State for Asia-Pacific, and David Matas, a human rights lawyer who specialized in mass atrocities, began their investigation that the movement truly gained traction.

Kilgour and Matas shared two essential qualities: both were deeply moral men, and neither was afraid to confront something almost too horrific to believe—something no government or institution would ever willingly admit to.

In July 2006, less than two months after the panel at Auschwitz, they released the first serious report on China's organ-harvesting operations. Their conclusion was chilling: large-scale organ seizures from unwilling Falun Gong practitioners were indeed taking place across China.

A revised version of the report was released early the next year.[9] The thirty-three pieces of evidence are reprinted in full below:

General Considerations

1. China is a systematic human rights violator. The overall pattern of violations makes it harder to dismiss than any one claimed violation.
2. The Government of China has reduced, substantially, financing of the health system. Organ transplants are a major source of funds for this system, replacing the lost government funding.
3. The Government of China has given the military the green light to raise money for arms privately. The military is heavily involved in organ transplants to raise money for itself.
4. Corruption in China is a major problem. There is huge money to be made from transplants and a lack of state control over corruption.

Considerations Specific to Organ Harvesting

5. Technology has developed to the point where organ harvesting of innocents has become possible. Developments in transplant surgery in China fall prey to the cruelty, the corruption, and the repression which pervades China.
6. China harvests the organs of prisoners sentenced to death without their consent. The Falun Gong constitute a prison population who the Chinese authorities vilify, dehumanize, depersonalize, and marginalize even more than executed prisoners sentenced to death for criminal offences.
7. There is no organized system of organ donation in China. There is a Chinese cultural aversion to organ donation.
8. Wait times for organ transplants in China are incredibly short, a matter of days. Everywhere else in the world, wait times are measured in months and years.

9. Hospital websites post self-incriminating information boasting short wait times for all high-cost organs.
10. Donor recipients whom we have interviewed tell us about the secrecy with which transplant surgery is undertaken and the heavy involvement of the military. Information given to patients is kept to a minimum. Transplants are performed in military hospitals and even in civilian hospitals, by military personnel.
11. There is huge money to be made in China from transplants. Prices charged to foreigners range from $30,000.00 US for corneas to $180,000.00 US for a liver-kidney combination.
12. There are no Chinese transplant ethics separate from the laws which govern transplants. China does not have a self-governing disciplinary body for transplant professionals.
13. There are huge gaps in foreign transplant ethics. It is rare for foreign transplant ethics to deal specifically with transplant tourism, contact with Chinese transplant professionals, or transplants from executed prisoners.
14. The practice of selling organs in China was legal until July 1, 2006. Even today, the new law banning the sale of organs is not enforced.
15. Foreign transplant legislation everywhere is territorial. It is not illegal for a foreigner in any country to go to China, benefit from a transplant that would be illegal in their country of origin, and then return home.
16. Many states have travel advisories, warning their citizens of the perils involved in traveling to one country or another, but no government has posted a travel advisory about organ transplants in China.
17. Organ transplantation surgery relies on anti-rejection drugs. China imports these drugs from the major pharmaceutical companies. No state prohibits export to China of anti-rejection drugs used for organ transplant patients.

18. Some state-administered health plans pay for health care abroad in the amount that would be paid if the care were administered in a patient's home country, or pay for after-care of patients who obtain transplants abroad. Among countries where this is the case, none prohibit payment should patients obtain organ transplants in China.

Considerations Specific to Falun Gong

19. The Communist Party of China, for no apparent reason other than totalitarian paranoia, sees Falun Gong as an ideological threat to its existence. Yet, objectively, Falun Gong is just a set of exercises with a spiritual component.
20. The threat the Communist Party perceives from the Falun Gong community has led to a policy of persecution. Persecution of the Falun Gong in China is officially decided and decreed.
21. Falun Gong practitioners are victims of extreme vilification. The official Chinese position on Falun Gong is that it is "an evil cult." Yet, Falun Gong shares none of the characteristics of a cult.
22. Falun Gong practitioners are victims of systematic torture and ill treatment. While the claims of organ harvesting of Falun Gong practitioners have been met with doubt, there is no doubt about this torture.
23. Falun Gong practitioners have been arrested in huge numbers; they are detained without trial or charge until they renounce Falun Gong beliefs.
24. There are thousands of named, identified Falun Gong practitioners who died as a result of torture. If the Government of China is willing to kill large numbers of Falun Gong

practitioners through torture, it is not that hard to imagine they would be willing to do the same through organ harvesting.

25. Many practitioners, in attempt to protect their families and communities, have not identified themselves once arrested. The unidentified are a particularly vulnerable population.
26. Falun Gong practitioners in prison are systematically blood-tested and physically examined. Yet, because they are also systematically tortured, this testing cannot be motivated by concerns over their health.
27. Traditional sources of transplants—executed prisoners, donors, and the brain-dead—come nowhere near accounting for the total number of transplants in China. The only other identified source which can explain the skyrocketing transplant numbers is Falun Gong practitioners.
28. The money to be made from organ transplants has led to the creation of dedicated facilities, specializing in organ transplants. The Chinese authorities must have confidence that there exists, into the foreseeable future, a readily-available source of organs from people who are alive now and will be dead tomorrow. Who are these people? A large prison population of Falun Gong practitioners provides an answer.
29. In a few cases, between death and cremation, family members of Falun Gong practitioners were able to see the mutilated corpses of their loved ones; organs had been removed.
30. We had callers phoning hospitals throughout China posing as family members of persons who needed organ transplants. In a wide variety of locations, those who were called asserted that Falun Gong practitioners (reputedly healthy because of their exercise regimen) were the source of the organs. We have recordings and telephone bills for these calls.

31. We interviewed the ex-wife of a surgeon from Sujiatun who had said her husband personally removed the corneas from approximately two thousand anesthetized Falun Gong prisoners at Sujiatun hospital, in Shenyang City, in northeast China, during the two-year period before October 2003. Her testimony was credible to us.
32. There have been two investigations independent from our own which have addressed the same question we have addressed, whether there is organ harvesting of Falun Gong practitioners in China, one by Kirk Allison of the University of Minnesota, another by European Parliament Vice President Edward McMillan-Scott. Both have come to the same conclusion we did. These independent investigations corroborate our own conclusion.
33. The Government of China has responded to the first version of our report in an unpersuasive way. Mostly, the responses have been attacks on the Falun Gong. The fact the Government of China, with all the resources and information at its disposal—resources and information we do not have—was not able to contradict our report, suggests that our conclusions are accurate.

For anyone paying attention—and there was a growing number of us—the Kilgour-Matas report was a bombshell. More importantly, the evidence presented in the Davids' report was impossible to dismiss. As that body of evidence grew throughout 2006, I came to a sobering realization, one that was only reinforced in the years that followed: It was real. It was beyond tragic. And it had to be stopped.

CHAPTER 2

A LONG HISTORY OF MURDER

THE CCP'S RESPONSE: DENIAL, SLANDER, AND DISMISSAL

Still, I had to ask myself: Could the CCP *really* be that cruel? Could they really be selling body parts for profit?

Soon, more evidence came to light.

In late 2006, David Kilgour reported on a story about a former Chinese military surgeon who had eight Chinese citizens killed to supply a single foreign patient with a new kidney. "The incredible thing is that the doctor would . . . go down the names on sheets of paper looking for blood types and tissue types and so on, and he [the patient] would point at names on the list. The doctor would then go away and come back with organs," said Kilgour.[1]

While conducting research in Asia, Kilgour interviewed a man (name and nationality withheld) who received a kidney transplant at Shanghai No. 1 People's Hospital in 2003. The man said that his surgeon was Dr. Tan Jianming, Secretary General of the Chinese Research Society of Dialysis and Transplantation. Dr.

Tan also held top posts in a number of Chinese military and civilian hospitals.

The patient suffered from an antibody condition that made it difficult to find a suitable kidney. Over eight days, four separate kidneys were brought to him and tested, said Kilgour. When none of those worked, three months later, he tried another four, the last of which was a fit. The man was later transferred to No. 85 Hospital of the People's Liberation Army to convalesce.

Dr. Tan told the man explicitly that these organs came from executed Chinese prisoners, and that at least some of the organs had been harvested secretly, against the donors' will.

"I am certain that at least some of these were Falun Gong practitioners who never went near a court, who were never convicted of anything," said Kilgour.[2]

All of the reporting was credible, but no one had found a smoking gun—and what would such a thing even be?

Of course, with forced organ harvesting, a smoking gun is almost an impossibility for a simple reason: no forced organ harvesting system would allow the "donors" to survive. For this crime, the crime scene is the CCP's vast, brutal system of incarceration, where people disappear all the time, and the operating room, meticulously wiped clean after each harvest. In a very real sense, the absence of survivors is the signature of this criminal enterprise's success. (At this point, it would be many years before a survivor made it out to the West to tell his story.)

At that point, there was no real response from the Party either. In fact, there has never been a response that addresses the substance of the allegations. The tactic has always been the same: attack the messenger (in this case, the Falun Gong trying to bring attention to these crimes against humanity) and demonize them. The message was simple: Falun Gong is a "heretical religion." Period. End of story. It was entirely consistent with the CCP's broader vilification campaign against Falun Gong practitioners.

There was one exception, of sorts. Following allegations that a particular hospital was being used to detain people for organ harvesting, the CCP announced it would welcome outside observers to come and see for themselves, mere weeks after the allegations were made. They came, and, unsurprisingly, found nothing. Everything appeared legitimate. The visitors left saying, "I don't see any evidence of organ harvesting. Case closed."

It was, in hindsight, a Potemkin village operation—a meticulously staged ruse to conceal the truth. But at the time, it worked.

It's very difficult for people who grow up in a free society, as I did, to truly understand what it's like to live under a totalitarian regime, or even an authoritarian one. This was something I had to come to terms with myself, and it took a long time to get there.

The key to understanding the Chinese Communist Party, or any totalitarian system, is recognizing that there is no such thing as civil society under totalitarianism. In the United States and free societies around the world, when people see a need, they organize themselves. They form voluntary associations to address specific issues. Those associations and organizations become the foundation for a vibrant civil society. This is what Alexis de Tocqueville found most remarkable about America and what inspired his belief in the country's great future.

In a totalitarian society like communist China, which, historically speaking, is a relatively new and still poorly understood political innovation, the state controls everything. Anything that even suggests independence from state authority is either crushed or co-opted. Such a society can't function any other way. There is no space for a civil society because its very existence would threaten the Party's absolute control.

What makes totalitarianism distinct is that it allows for no independent organizing principle outside the state. Unless the system collapses under its own weight, there are no mechanisms for ordinary people to build something new or self-sustaining on any meaningful scale. Of course, there are always the extraordinarily brave dissidents who find ways to resist, knowing full well that the cost, if discovered, could be death. They exist, and they matter, but their courage comes at an almost unimaginable price.

The communist totalitarian system functions as a *political pathocracy*, which psychiatrist Andrzej Łobaczewski described in *Political Ponerology*, a book he wrote after Poland came under Soviet occupation. With other dissidents with expertise in the area, he traced what happened to Iron Curtain societies as they became increasingly more dominated by communists. In this system, he determined, power doesn't rise through merit or moral character; it concentrates in the hands of those with sociopathic and psychopathic traits—people devoid of empathy, integrity, or restraint—because those are the qualities most rewarded by the system itself. To be clear, this doesn't mean that *everybody*, or even most people in the system, are this way, but it does mean that such people rise to the top. And in terrorizing people around them along the way, they have a deforming effect on society, as normal people develop necessary adaptations to living in a pathocracy.

HOW STATE VIOLENCE HAS SHAPED THE CCP'S MODERN STRATEGY

The twentieth and twenty-first centuries have borne witness to the results of this pathocracy time and again. China's organ-harvesting industry is entirely consistent with the Chinese Communist Party's long history of killing its own people, as violence has been woven into its structure from the very beginning. The Party itself has killed more of its own citizens than any regime in recorded history.

The Great Leap Forward was just one of many campaigns launched in the name of "strengthening" China that instead led to mass death. Under that policy, individuals were forced to divert their labor and resources toward the smelting of steel, often in makeshift backyard furnaces. Fields were abandoned, crops failed, and famine spread across the country.

The unintended effect was the creation of a kind of cannibal culture. Mao Zedong's Great Leap Forward (1958–1962) was supposed to be a glorious sprint into communist paradise. Instead, it became the single greatest man-made slaughter in human history. In four short years, blind ideology, forced collectivization, and psychotic agricultural "innovations" starved at least 45 million Chinese to death—some scholars say 55–60 million. People ate grass, bark, clay—even their own children. Cadres beat farmers who hid a single grain. Bodies piled in ditches; entire counties went silent. Mao knew, yet doubled down, calling the dying "fertilizer for socialism." Mao's ideological hysteria, enforced by terror, turned the world's most populous nation into a graveyard of shattered families and hollow promises, all in the name of "progress."

The sheer disregard for human life was staggering.

The Cultural Revolution, another of China's cataclysmic policy failures, followed the same pattern of ideological madness and mass violence. In the late 1950s, Mao Zedong was seeking to consolidate power around himself. Even many within his own ranks questioned his earlier campaigns, such as the Great Leap Forward, and he knew his authority was slipping.

To reassert control, Mao turned to the youth. In 1966, he empowered the Chinese Red Guard—a youth paramilitary group—to wage a crusade against China's own history and culture, in the name of purifying it for communism. In particular, he wanted to purify it of the "four olds"—old Ideas, old Culture, old Customs, and old Habits—which he believed were remnants of China's feudal past and obstacles to revolutionary transformation. In practice, the campaign targeted traditional beliefs, classical literature and art, religious practices, social etiquette, and everyday cultural traditions. The effort to purge these "olds" led to the widespread destruction of temples, books, and artifacts, the renaming of streets and institutions, and the persecution of teachers and intellectuals. To be educated, to think independently, to hold to tradition—any of these could mark you for destruction. Those who pledged loyalty and "struggled" against others might survive, especially if they were young. For many, joining the Red Guard was both a privilege and a survival tactic.

It was an era of extraordinary violence. Teachers, intellectuals, and ordinary citizens were publicly humiliated, beaten, and often killed for the smallest perceived offenses—teaching the wrong thing, owning forbidden books, or hiding an heirloom. The violence was ritualized and theatrical. People were forced to renounce everything they believed in, confess to imaginary crimes, and beg for mercy in front of their communities. Those who admitted to being "evil" might be spared, but often only to live mutilated or in lifelong shame. Historians estimate that around six million people were killed during that decade.

In unleashing this terror, Mao discovered how to weaponize the most ruthless elements of society. He promoted the people with no moral boundaries and elevated them through the ranks, creating a mania—a revolution that devoured itself.

Most people, of course, tried to stay out of it, but that was nearly impossible. Mao's genius, if one can call it that, was in forcing everyone into complicity. Under constant fear, people were driven to denounce family members, neighbors, even close friends, just to survive.

Recently, viewers of the Netflix adaptation of Liu Cixin's *The Three-Body Problem* were treated to a depiction of the reality of the Cultural Revolution in full form. The show opens with the scene of a public struggle session in which a young woman is forced to watch as her father is beaten to death for refusing to betray his scientific principles. Unable to intervene, she becomes complicit through silence—an example of how the Communist Party shattered moral agency by turning survival into acquiescence. That trauma shapes her worldview: years later, when she encounters an alien civilization with hostile intentions, she responds with a hollow, nihilistic invitation for them to come.

The scene captures how totalitarian violence can drive even idealistic people into profound moral despair.

In such a system, even those who were not psychopathic were compelled to act, at least to some extent, as if they were. To save yourself, you might have to betray someone else, and in doing so, you lose the moral high ground. The system won either way.

This pattern repeats in every totalitarian society: citizens are cornered into no-win choices, forced to pick the lesser evil, and in doing so, they internalize the system's corruption. It's not an accident; it's the inevitable outcome of a structure that places no value on human life.

The persecution of Falun Gong, and the use of its practitioners for organ harvesting fit seamlessly into that lineage, not as an aberration but as the logical continuation of the Party's contempt for humanity, albeit in a way that could remain hidden for years.

CHAPTER 3

THE CCP INSTRUMENTALIZES EVERYTHING

COMMUNIST PARTY SUPREMACY

Imagine a society where human life has no intrinsic value, and where a person is worth only the sum of their physical parts, or the utility of their knowledge, or the influence they can offer.

Imagine a society where a supremacist ruling body—the Party—assigns each individual a measurable worth, a kind of social credit score. Elites are protected, enriched, and empowered. Entire classes of people are targeted for repression or elimination, according to their political designation.

Imagine a society where everything is instrumentalized—health care, education, law, even human beings themselves.

That society is Communist China today.

And given the state's ideological underpinnings, none of its horrific outcomes should be surprising. Communism is a materialist ideology. It recognizes no accountability to any higher power, moral or divine. It sees human existence as an endless struggle between oppressor and oppressed. In its original Marxist formulation, the working class battles the owning class; once the workers achieve "class consciousness" and recognize their oppression, they rise up to replace their oppressors.

The critical point is this: there is no higher power than the Party. The Party *is* the higher power. The preservation of everything else, including human life itself, is secondary to the preservation of the Party.

In that sense, it functions as a kind of morally corrosive quasi-religion—one in which the Party assumes the role of judge, jury, and executioner. Ultimate moral authority resides entirely within it. From there, instrumentalization becomes inevitable. Instrumentalization is the act of reducing a person, group, idea, institution, or even an event to a mere tool or weapon to serve a specific agenda—stripping it of its inherent dignity, reality, truth, or autonomy. Everything is justified in the name of the "greater good," and the greater good, of course, is anything that helps the Party survive and thrive.

The Party is never wrong. But, of course, life under the CCP is rife with difficulties and problems. And someone has to be blamed for the endless failures the Party produces, some explanation provided to the masses, lest they one day realize the true culprit.

The logic is simple: Identify whatever most threatens the Party's continued dominance and make it the enemy. From the outside, that makes the United States of America the perfect target. It's the world's largest superpower and, for all its flaws, it represents freedom, individual rights, and personal responsibility—the very values that expose the moral bankruptcy of the Chinese Communist Party. Those traits make it, in the Party's eyes, the ideal external aggressor, the ultimate scapegoat.

BLACK CLASSES AND THE LOGIC OF ENEMY DESIGNATION

However, the Party needs internal enemies as well—people who can see through the illusion of the Party's supremacy or whose mere existence contradicts it. The Party fears them even more than the external adversaries and deals with them far more violently.

Communism is deeply identitarian in this sense. Once you're marked as a member of a "black class," there's little you can do to change your fate. You might survive if you pledge absolute loyalty to the Party—denouncing your family, struggling against your friends, proving your devotion again and again—but that requires a level of moral compromise most people can hardly imagine. For a psychopath, though, it's quite easy.

Black classes (黑五类) are identity groups that the CCP targeted for persecution, notably during the Cultural Revolution:

Landlords (地主): Anyone who had owned even a modest amount of land before 1949 was labeled an "exploiter." Their children and grandchildren were automatically "black" for generations, denied education, jobs, and often beaten or killed.

Rich Peasants (富农): Farmers who had hired a little labor or owned slightly more than average were branded class enemies. Entire families were starved, humiliated in struggle sessions, or sent to die in labor camps.

Rightists (右派): Intellectuals, teachers, or anyone who dared whisper the mild criticism of the Party in 1957's Hundred Flowers Campaign—an effort to allow the public to voice criticism of the Party that ended when the government cracked down on critics. Over 550,000 were labeled rightists; many were tortured to death or driven to suicide during the Cultural Revolution.

These labels turned millions into sub-humans overnight—legally discriminated against, publicly degraded, and frequently murdered with official approval.

But the crucial element of the CCP's view on black classes is not simply that they are targeted for elimination, re-education, or persecution, but that they are systematically instrumentalized.

They have to be *made* useful, which means useful to the Party.

Landlords were among the first to be instrumentalized by the party. The perfect scapegoat for centuries of peasant suffering. In the early 1950s land-reform terror campaign, the Party orchestrated hundreds of thousands of public "struggle sessions" where landlords were beaten to death or forced to confess imaginary crimes in front of frenzied crowds. This wasn't justice, it was theater. The spectacle turned poor peasants into willing participants in murder, binding them psychologically to the Party through shared guilt and stolen property. Once the landlords were exterminated or broken, their children inherited the black label forever, creating a permanent underclass that reminded everyone: "Cross the Party and your grandchildren will still pay."

Likewise, rich peasants were used as the warning example during collectivization and the Great Leap Forward. The Party labeled them "capitalist roaders in the village" to justify seizing everything and forcing everyone into people's communes. When the inevitable famine came, the regime blamed "rich peasant sabotage" for the mass starvation, while cadres were actually stealing grain. Rich peasants were paraded, tortured, and often killed first, sending the message to middle and poor peasants: "Even modest success makes you an enemy. Stay poor and obedient, or you're next."

This tactic has been used ever since, at every level of society, and new "black classes" like the Falun Gong have since been established. Now, in the twenty-first century, it's impossible to talk about how the CCP came to instrumentalize Falun Gong practitioners without first talking about the health-care system in China.

The health-care system in China is perhaps the purest, most direct reflection of the Party's ultimate goal: self-preservation. It is a literal life-extension industry for the Party elite.

There are actually two systems in China—one for the elites, and another for everyone else. The elite system is excellent. The public system is rudimentary, underfunded, and riddled with corruption, with much of the funding that moves through bureaucratic channels siphoned off by officials at various levels before it ever reaches patients.

UTILITARIAN BIOETHICS

China's two health-care systems are not merely the byproduct of a corrupt organization or a tale of haves and have-nots. It has been engineered, like all systems in China, by the CCP. It is part and parcel of the Party's approach to health care for the general population, which they view through the lens of utilitarian bioethics, an ideology that by nature devalues individual life.

Traditional medical ethics, rooted in the Hippocratic principle of "do no harm," is patient-centered. Its purpose is to help the person in front of the physician, using whatever tools and knowledge are available. Medicine, in that sense, is an art grounded in compassion and individual responsibility.

Utilitarian bioethics turns that on its head. It views health in terms of statistical outcomes and population-level goals. The guiding idea is "the greatest good for the greatest number" (sometimes described as "the greatest happiness for the greatest number"), with the caveat that the Party always comes first because without the Party, there is no state. If improving the overall picture means sacrificing a few, the sacrifice is justified. Many might call that reasonable—after all, every policy carries some cost—but the consequences of utilitarian bioethics are profound.

The difference lies in what is valued. Under a utilitarian model, human beings become variables in an equation. The second-order effects—the erosion of empathy, the normalization of sacrifice—are immense but largely invisible.

The COVID-19 years revealed the consequences of this mindset with brutal clarity. In China, the government's draconian lockdowns—people welded into their homes, food passed through metal slots—were extreme expressions of utilitarian bioethics. The policy was irrational, but it made sense within the CCP's worldview: a top-down system obsessed with control and indifferent to human suffering in pursuit of its "zero COVID" objective. The regime had both the ideology and the mechanisms to enforce it.

That is utilitarian bioethics in its purest form: sacrificing individual welfare for a population-level target, implemented by a state willing to bear, or impose, the human cost. The personal element disappears. Everything becomes transactional, or instrumentalized.

The problem with "the greatest good for the greatest number" is that someone must decide where the line of acceptable harm lies. In a totalitarian system, that line barely exists. As long as the population does not rebel, almost any level of suffering can be justified.

The Hippocratic model, by contrast, preserves individual agency. It demands that practitioners engage creatively and compassionately with the person before them, rather than treating patients as data points on a bell curve. It represents a fundamentally different way of thinking about human life.

In a communist society, the utilitarian model reigns supreme, in essence, by definition. It is the moral logic behind the infamous quip often attributed to Stalin: "In order to make an omelet, you have to break a few eggs." The idea is not unique to China, and, indeed, we are already seeing these ideas creep into the mainstream in far freer societies. But China has taken it much further, pushing utilitarian bioethics to its extreme conclusion.

The communist model runs on systemic graft. The Party sets strategic objectives, which are implemented in different ways across society. Success is measured not by ethics or outcomes but by how effectively those objectives are fulfilled. Profit, power, and self-enrichment are tolerated, even encouraged, so long as they serve the Party's broader goals. There is no rule of law in the conventional sense; there is only compliance with Party directives. Anything is permissible.

The dangers of this overly controlled, engineered approach to how people should live become abundantly clear when we take a broader look at how the CCP has implemented it. The one-child policy is a prime example.

The precise reasoning behind the policy is unclear—perhaps they read Paul Erlich's 1968 *The Population Bomb* and decided to believe it. The idea that there are too many people on the planet and humanity is in danger of destroying itself captured the imaginations of many people in the middle of the twentieth century. Some still believe it today, even though it has led to some of the worst outcomes imaginable.

Regardless of its internal logic at the time, China believed that the growth of the population needed to be slowed, and in 1979, the Party instituted the one-child policy to do it. The policy was in place until 2015.

There were other advantages—from the Party's perspective. Traditionally, Chinese families are large; it's a deeply family-oriented culture. The family is the core structure where people find comfort, loyalty, and support. A strong family unit creates natural independence because people prioritize family over the Party. Understanding the inherent threat posed by a society with a strong family structure, the Party sought to undo it.

Families were limited to a single child, and local governments were given quotas to enforce the rule. If families in a district exceeded the limit, the local officials responsible could lose privileges, or see their share of graft reduced. There were always incentives to ensure compliance.

The consequences were devastating. First, birth rates fell sharply. Second, abortion was promoted as a social good. Third, and most horrific, the state carried out forced abortions on a massive scale. There were countless cases of women being coerced or physically forced to terminate pregnancies. Selective abortions were also common, as families tended to prefer sons over daughters.

The result was a profound gender imbalance—millions more men than women—and a shortage of young people needed to sustain the aging population. Now China faces a vast demographic hole: too few young people to care for the old, and a social system unable to support its own weight. Beginning in 2016, to counter the effects of the one-child policy, the Chinese government replaced it with a two-child policy. When it became clear that the change had little effect, the state expanded the limit again in 2021 to a three-child policy, essentially raising the ceiling every five years as demographic pressures worsened. These shifts reflected the Party's growing alarm over shrinking workforce numbers, low fertility, and the long-term economic strain of an imbalanced population structure. In the end, this may prove to be one of the greatest threats to the Party's long-term stability.

There is no clear solution.

You could argue that the CCP's One-Child Policy wasn't entirely about population control—it was a deliberate, decades-long war on the traditional Chinese family, which is the most basic traditional unit of all human societies. By criminalizing brothers and sisters, by sending goon squads to drag pregnant mothers for forced abortions and sterilizations, by turning grandparents, neighbors, even husbands against wives through terror and bounties, the Party systematically shattered the multi-generational family that had been China's core moral and social unit for millennia. Filial piety? Obliterated. Family loyalty? Replaced with loyalty to the Party alone. The goal was crystal clear: atomize society, leave every individual isolated, dependent, and obedient only to the state.

The CCP doesn't see its citizens as individuals with inherent dignity, but rather as raw material. Xi Jinping has compared China's human talent to "oil in the ground" that must be drilled, refined, and burned for national power. That same logic runs the vast slave-labor empire: laogai (camps with convicted criminals doing forced labor), "re-education through labor" camps (abolished in 2013, but arguably just moved into different parts of the system), Xinjiang factories where Uyghurs and dissidents are worked literally to death making your Christmas lights, personal protective equipment (PPE), solar panels, everything. When a worker collapses, the body is discarded.

Human life, in such a monstrous system, is just another resource to be used, exhausted, and discarded.

CHAPTER 4

WHAT TARGETING FALUN GONG REVEALS ABOUT THE NATURE OF THE CCP

XIAOFU

One morning in late 1999, the workers of Shengyang Heavy Machine Factory were met with a surprise. Instead of relaying the usual announcements, the company's loudspeakers were on the warpath. "Traitor!" they yelled. "Evil!" they screamed. The object of their malice was junior sales manager Li Weixun. The workers who knew her could not believe their ears.

To those Shenyang Factory workers who were old enough to remember, the day was an eerie throwback to the sixties and seventies, to the Cultural Revolution. Only a few months earlier, Weixun, or Xiaofu as she is known to friends, was by all accounts viewed as a model citizen.

"Mao Zedong said that we should serve the people. I was an obedient child, so I listened, followed the Party. I wanted to be a good person," she says from her apartment in New York City.

She arrived in the United States in September 2005, a UN-protected refugee.

After Mao's death, she got a college degree, married her childhood sweetheart, and gave birth to a son, Yiping. She took work in sales and marketing. She was a Communist Party member until that morning in 1999, when the loudspeakers announced she had been sacked from the factory and purged from the Party ranks. But, Xiaofu was not there to face her accusers.

She was being detained by police in a deep, underground cell where she was being severely beaten and subject to around-the-clock propaganda videos. Police demanded that she sign a little piece of paper, after which all of this ill-treatment would go away. How had Xiaofu so offended the system that she had previously embraced?

In 1996, Xiaofu discovered Falun Gong, the spiritual discipline that was spreading like wildfire across China. It changed her life. An illness that had plagued her for years was gone, and she felt uplifted. Millions of Chinese were experiencing something similar.

"She changed a lot. She was getting rid of a lot of heavy burdens [and] . . . was looking at the world in a totally different way. There was more love in the family," says her son Yiping, who later started to practice himself.

Everything changed on July 20, 1999.

"I went to the practice site as usual, only to find that we were not allowed to practice anymore. Many police came to say that it was banned. My first response was disbelief. Such a good practice, how can you outlaw us?" recalls Xiaofu.

Within hours, hundreds of thousands of practitioners around the country were heading to their local governments to appeal the decision, a directive from then-Chinese dictator Jiang Zemin. Xiaofu and Yiping were among them.

Mother and son were arrested and taken to a large stadium. They were shown videos slandering Falun Gong and police demanded they sign a document certifying that they would give up practicing. They refused and were released with a "warning."

Two months later, Xiaofu was arrested again after going to appeal to the national government in Beijing. Police escorted her into custody back in her hometown. It was soon after this arrest that the Shengyang Heavy Machine Factory loudspeakers attacked her in her absence. Despite beatings and brainwashing tactics, Xiaofu continued to refuse to renounce Falun Gong. It took four months and 20,000 Yuan (USD $2,500) paid in extortion money for her family to secure her release.

Xiaofu made up her mind to expose what had happened to her and to other practitioners, some of whom had met even more grisly fates. She became active distributing printed materials that debunked the state hate-propaganda that was saturating the Chinese media. It was her moral obligation, she insists.

On June 10, 1999, the 610 Office (named for the day of its creation) was formed by then General Secretary of the CCP Jiang Zemin with a primary goal to destroy the Falun Gong. This new security agency was managed by high-ranking CCP officials to ensure autonomy and so that it outranked other departments. As a CCP-led office with no written law or mandate, the 610 Office was an extra-legal organization that could operate with impunity, designed to ensure that the Falun Gong persecution program, which many officials were not enthusiastic about, was implemented with zeal. In May of 2000, the 610 Office laid a trap for Xiaofu at her home, but friends were able to alert her ahead of time. She left, expecting that it might be for good. Whenever she called, Yiping recalls, he was too afraid to mention her name, lest she be tracked down.

In mid-January 2002, almost two years after she left her family, the 610 Office raided an underground materials site, housing a cache of leaflets exposing the atrocities committed against practitioners.

Xiaofu was one of the practitioners picked up. She was interrogated and tortured for ninety-six hours, leaving her partially paralyzed from the waist down. By mid-February, still in detention, her arms were swollen black and blue. In early March, totally paralyzed from the waist down, she was sent to hospital. By mid-March, she was catatonic, and doctors deemed her terminally ill. She was released to her family, the police forcing them to pay another 50,000 Yuan (just over USD $6,000 at the time). Even then, police kept her under constant surveillance.

Incredibly, over the next twenty days, Xiaofu began to recover, being careful to not alert the police to her increased strength and mobility. She credits this miracle to focusing on Falun Gong teachings in her mind, and to middle-of-the-night meditations.

Gradually the police let their guard down. With the help of her older brother, Xiaofu escaped. Family members were interrogated, beaten, and put under house arrest as punishment.

"When a person is faced with a choice between a family and spiritual beliefs, it's like a choice between losing your left arm or losing your right arm," she says, with tears in her eyes.

None of Xiaofu's family members have escaped persecution, even the non-practitioners. Nine of them were either arrested or forced to leave their homes to avoid police. Party officials from the Machine Factory pressured Xiofu's husband, who worked there as well, to seek a divorce. He asked her for one on two occasions, but in the end, love prevailed—he could not do it.

Yiping, refusing to sign the required pledge against Falun Gong, went to engineering school only because of his father's personal relationship with the university dean. Yiping practiced in secret. For two years, one of his dorm mates spied on him.

Given her circumstances and the pressure on her family, Xiaofu decided that leaving China was the best option.

"In hiding, I couldn't really visit family members in their homes. They were worried sick about my safety. Other practitioners also told me that that way I could expose the persecution to the public," she says.

Xiaofu's older brother obtained passports for his sister and several others. On August 8, 2002, she received a panicked phone call: Someone had exposed the operation. The next day, she flew to Bangkok to safety. Her brother, however, was sentenced to eight years for "disrupting the implementation of laws."

In Thailand, the UN accepted Xiaofu as a refugee and began the process of finding her a permanent home. Almost three years later, after graduating from university and now under the radar of the 610 Office, Yiping joined his mother. Their reunion was short lived. Not two months after Yiping's arrival, Xiaofu received papers to resettle in America.

Upon arrival, her message to other persecuted practitioners was humble and heartbreaking: "Don't give up."[1]

Xiaofu was the first Falun Gong refugee resettled in America that I am aware of, and among the earliest to escape what would become a decades-long campaign of persecution and eradication of Falun Gong practitioners by the Chinese Communist Party. Many others would follow in her footsteps, but an untold number would never even have the opportunity to try to make it out. Xiaofu, like many Falun Gong practitioners, was not motivated by self-preservation alone, but by a deep desire to tell her fellow countrymen the truth about Falun Gong, the persecution, and the CCP. In explaining the realities of Falun Gong, the truth about the CCP, and encouraging people to quit the party and its affiliated organizations, they arguably constitute the largest (grassroots) peaceful civil disobedience movement in existence.

FALUN GONG: EMERGENCE AND PERSECUTION

When the practice of Falun Gong first emerged in the 1990s, it did so as traditional Chinese health disciplines, collectively dubbed "qigong" in their modern versions, were becoming popular again. They were largely tolerated by the Chinese government.

In the West, we tend to view the mind, body, and spirit as separate elements. For the spirit, we have religion; for the body, sport; and for the mind, education. In the Eastern sense, whether in traditional India, China, or elsewhere, single systems, or "cultivation practices," often encompassed all of these aspects at once.

Falun Gong is one such practice. It has a physical component involving exercises and meditation, a mental component grounded in study of the teachings, and a spiritual component focused on individual moral improvement.

Many of these practices are ancient, passed down for generations from teacher to student. A teacher might guide one person or a small handful, who may or may not later teach others. Over time, these traditions continue quietly, often known only to those within them. There are tens of thousands of such lineages in the world today—most completely unknown to the broader public.

Each teacher typically refines or adapts the system slightly. Li Hongzhi, the originator of Falun Gong, as I understand it, made certain adjustments to make his practice more accessible to a wider audience, and he began teaching Falun Gong publicly in 1992.

At that time, China's health-care system had largely collapsed under the weight of corruption, utilitarian bioethics, and the widening gap between elite and public care. Many people were turning to traditional methods to restore their health and strengthen their spirit. A state-run organization called the China Qigong Research Society served as the official umbrella for all recognized qigong practices. It collected dues from participants to ensure each group's alignment with the system, all the way up the chain of command.

Li Hongzhi introduced Falun Gong under this structure and taught it for two years to large audiences—often a few thousand students at a time.

He then published "Zhuan Falun," the main text of Falun Gong, and announced that he would no longer teach in large public settings. Instead, he encouraged those who had benefited from the practice to share it freely with others.

Falun Gong has extensive teachings but relatively few what one might describe as "rules." The reason for this is that a key principle of Falun Gong is that one must find one's own understanding, one's own path, in applying the teachings. What I loosely describe as "rules" are actually common understandings I believe most, if not all, Falun Gong practitioners would agree on:

The core principles of the universe are Truthfulness, Compassion, and Forbearance.

One cannot use Falun Gong to enrich oneself financially.

One cannot coerce others to practice.

There is no worship of the Teacher or Master.

A further expectation is that each practitioner must understand and apply the teachings for themselves. No one can practice on another's behalf. A common trait among practitioners is humility in how they describe their understanding. They might say, "My understanding of Falun Gong is . . . " as a way of distinguishing personal insight from the teachings themselves.

It is a deeply individual practice. There is no membership list or formal organization. What defines a Falun Gong practitioner is living by the teachings, not belonging to a group.

It all sounds harmless, indeed, even positive. The Party did not see it that way. Taken together, it fosters an unusual degree of personal agency. Practitioners strive to live truthfully. They are serious about moral cultivation and not easily swayed by fear of ostracism or external pressure. If someone decides not to practice, others may feel regret, but no one will stop them. There are no dues, no hierarchies, no compulsion. It may be one of the few communities in the world that operates with so little external control.

While it was not created in opposition to the Party, everything about Falun Gong is anathema to the Marxist system. Falun Gong speaks to China's deep traditional culture—the very culture the CCP seeks to destroy. Falun Gong connects with ancient Buddhist and Daoist spirituality, and aligns with traditional Judeo-Christian values, while the CCP is deeply atheistic and allows for no higher authority than the Party itself. Falun Gong practitioners aspire to the principles of Truthfulness, Compassion, and Forbearance. The CCP rules by lies, violence, and total intolerance of anything outside its control.

The CCP doesn't believe in coexistence or win-win outcomes—only total domination. In a communist society, "truth" is whatever the Party requires it to be. People must behave as though that truth is real, and some may even come to believe it. But Falun Gong practitioners believe in *objective* truth, and that alone is a problem for the Party.

Perhaps for these very reasons—this reconnection with traditional beliefs and its health benefits—Falun Gong spread rapidly across China. By 1997, government estimates suggested that between 70 and 100 million people were practicing Falun Gong—*more* than the roughly 60 million members of the Communist Party at the time. All these things considered, for the supremacist organization that is the Party, I expect some came to view Falun Gong as an existential problem.

By 1999, an enormous number of people were deeply committed to the practice. It wasn't a hobby or social club; practitioners had integrated the teachings into their lives. At that point, the Party could no longer tolerate it.

In June 1999, Chinese Communist Party leader Jiang Zemin initiated a nationwide campaign to eradicate Falun Gong. The

610 Office, an extra-legal body under the control of high-ranking CCP officials, was established to lead the persecution. The Party mobilized the entire state apparatus—the media, the police, the education system, and every other arm of government—to "struggle" against practitioners.

But when Jiang launched the persecution, he didn't actually understand how Falun Gong worked. He simply perceived it as a threat to Party control, even though, as I would learn, a number of high-level communist leaders close to him disagreed with him on persecuting Falun Gong. Part of that threat, in the CCP's view, came from Falun Gong's association with what were known as the "Four Olds": old Ideas, old Culture, old Customs, and old Habits. Falun Gong honored traditional Chinese values and celebrated what was best and most humane in China's cultural heritage. The Party, of course, saw that as subversive.

The ensuing clampdown was swift and brutal.

The state deployed everything at its disposal. Propaganda outlets sprang into action, labeling Falun Gong a "heretical religion," and the practice was banned outright. Jiang Zemin even went so far as to give President Bill Clinton a book describing Falun Gong as dangerous and evil. The CCP also circulated this book among other world leaders.

A quick note of clarification: The best translation of China's official description of Falun Gong in official legal language is "unorthodox religious organization," per China law expert Clive Ansley, though I prefer to use "heretical religion," another credible translation, because it better reflects how the CCP views worldviews outside of its own.[2] The origin of the slanderous "cult" moniker (that many in the West have heard) stems from an October 25, 1999 interview Jiang Zemin did with the French newspaper *Le Figaro*.[3] It then appeared, in Chinese translation, as front page, above-the-fold headline news in all of China's major newspapers, and a day later a *People's Daily* editorial on the topic was reprinted by the Xinhua News Agency—the agency that sets the propaganda line for all Chinese media.

At first, the authorities believed they could "reform" practitioners quickly. But it proved far more difficult than expected. Local officials were held accountable for their "success" in reeducating practitioners: failure meant lost pay, reduced funding, or other punishments. This created a web of perverse incentives that encouraged abuse and brutality. In a totalitarian system like this, morality is irrelevant, and the only goal is to accomplish the task and avoid punishment. Questions of right and wrong don't enter the equation.

Before 2002, many ordinary Chinese citizens were still skeptical of the Party's narrative. That changed after a shocking incident in Tiananmen Square. A small group of people set themselves on fire in protest. The state media immediately claimed they were Falun Gong practitioners.

Any actual practitioner knew that this was impossible. Falun Gong is strictly nonviolent. Suicide or self-harm are explicitly forbidden.

The event, however, was filmed with suspicious precision by China Central Television (CCTV). Within hours, footage appeared across state media. There were odd inconsistencies like officials standing by with fire extinguishers, cameras positioned perfectly to capture the flames, and scenes edited together with cinematic precision.

Western outlets such as *The Washington Post* and *CNN* reported on the incident and later raised serious doubts about its authenticity. Evidence suggested it was a staged production, likely orchestrated by the state. Some witnesses claimed that at least one of the supposed "protesters" may have been killed on-site by police.

Regardless of the details, the propaganda impact was enormous. The footage flooded Chinese television screens. The message was clear: Falun Gong practitioners were dangerous fanatics. Many viewers believed it. The incident became one of the most successful propaganda operations in the CCP's modern history—turning public opinion decisively against Falun Gong and giving cover for the escalating persecution.

Yet these people weren't giving up their faith. They weren't saying, "Yes, Falun Gong is evil. Yes, I will help you reeducate other Falun Gong practitioners," as the Party expected.

The 610 Office was the game changer. It provided agents with sweeping authority to control resources, direct police, and enforce Jiang's orders. It showed local officials what was expected. Those who failed to implement directives were branded disloyal to the Party. The system was corrosive, spreading through every layer of society.

The office's creation was necessary, in the Party's eyes, because Falun Gong was everywhere—one in thirteen Chinese were practitioners prior to the 1999 ban. They were neighbors, colleagues, relatives. Even in a totalitarian state, ordinary people do not easily turn on those they know to be good. The regime needed an instrument of coercion backed by the highest authority—the Politburo Standing Committee—to force compliance among officials who might otherwise hesitate. Most people are not psychopaths; they don't naturally want to torture the innocent.

When the Party began arresting "leaders"—who weren't really leaders in any hierarchical sense, but coordinators of local practice sites—it made no difference. Beijing alone had some ten thousand practice sites in parks and public spaces. When one coordinator was taken away, another quietly stepped in. The structure of Falun Gong itself fostered personal agency; it could not simply be decapitated.

Here's what former US Ambassador-at-Large for International Religious Freedom Sam Brownback (who also served as US Senator and Governor of Kansas) told the world via video conference in the US Capitol, during 2025 events commemorating the beginnings of the Falun Gong persecution:

"I've worked with Falun Gong people for 20-25 years now, in different capacities, and the Chinese Communist Party just loathes this institution, this group. They hate them, and they treat them worse than anybody. And that's really saying something, because the Chinese Communist Party treats all religions poorly.

"I'm in Kansas right now, and . . . if you throw wheat on the soil in Kansas, it just grows. It's natural. Falun Gong is very natural to China and the Chinese mentality and the Chinese heart. And I think that's why the Communist Party so fears and does everything it possibly can to stomp out this faith, and they won't get it done, because it's physical man attacking a spiritual entity. It's the kingdom of man against the kingdom of God, and it won't succeed. You can cause a lot of harm in the process."[4]

AN UNWRITTEN RULE: BO XILAI AND THE ROOTS OF A FORCED ORGAN HARVESTING INDUSTRY

In truth, if one were to design a system to help people resist spiritual and psychological destruction under a totalitarian regime, it would look very much like Falun Gong.

That's when an unwritten rule emerged: all Falun Gong deaths in custody would be recorded as suicides. With that single policy, officials gained a license to kill. Around the same time, quotas for "reeducation" were introduced. The persecution intensified, partly because the Party still didn't understand what it was dealing with. Totalitarians have a totalitarian mindset—it's difficult for them to comprehend people who make their own decisions. Falun Gong practitioners choose how to live, how to practice, and how to conduct themselves morally.

The same mentality that produced the one-child policy—the belief that human life can be managed, optimized, or eliminated in the name of a collective good—also shaped the campaign against Falun Gong. When Jiang determined that Falun Gong must be eradicated, he initiated a nationwide competition among regional officials to see who could suppress the group most effectively.

In many ways, China's organ-harvesting industry grew out of the natural instincts of a totalitarian system: survival, subjugation, control, and instrumentalization. There was no grand plan at the beginning, only a series of perverse incentives that evolved into something monstrous.

How, exactly, it began is the subject of debate and speculation.

If you examine the timelines of events and the interwoven interests of the individuals involved, you could argue that it all started with one particularly brutal figure named Bo Xilai, the governor of Dalian, a port city in Liaoning Province, in the early 2000s. Around that time, a German anatomist named Gunther von Hagens was seeking a site for a factory that would specialize in the plastination of human bodies—a process that preserves corpses for medical study and public display. (His work later became the basis for the "Bodies" exhibitions that toured globally.) German authorities refused to allow him to build such a factory in Germany, but Bo Xilai offered to host it in Dalian.

Bo also had a close ally and police chief named Wang Lijun. Formerly the head of the Chongqing Public Security Bureau and the on-site Psychological Research Center in Liaoning Province from 2003 to 2008, Wang had conducted experiments on lethal injection methods that would allow organs to be removed for transplant before the victim died. His research also focused on minimizing the effects of execution drugs on transplant recipients.

Could this be where the modern system of forced organ harvesting in China began, under Bo Xilai and Wang Lijun? The pieces fit: Bo was ambitious, ruthless, and Wang was willing to innovate politically and technically to advance his standing. The timeline works, as well. Falun Gong persecution had begun in the late 1990s, just before Bo had built the plastination factory. An instrumentalization mentality would have led him to conclude that Falun Gong prisoners could be used as a source of bodies, which naturally progresses rapidly into organ harvesting, and by 2003, he'd engaged the psychopathic Wang Lijun to help make sure it was all running smoothly.

After 2004, Wang moved with Bo Xilai from Liaoning to Chongqing—they were very much a team, and in 2006, Wang received the Guanghua Science and Technology Foundation's "Innovation Special Contribution Award" for his work. In his acceptance speech, he openly referred to "thousands of on-site organ transplant cases" involving executed prisoners in which he and his team had participated.[5]

The two later became central figures in a dramatic political scandal. In March 2012, Wang Lijun sought refuge in a US Consulate in Chengdu after presenting evidence of corruption against Bo. Wang alleged that Bo was impeding a corruption investigation against his wife, Gu Kailai, who was implicated in the murder of a British Businessman, Neil Heywood. Bo responded by surrounding the consulate with armed police and demanding Wang's surrender, triggering an international incident. (Gu was later arrested for Heywood's murder, serving life in prison.)

According to reports, Wang may have revealed details of organ-harvesting operations to US officials during this brief stay inside the consulate, though he was ultimately denied asylum. Whatever the exact details, what *is* clear is that Wang Lijun was deeply involved in organ-harvesting research and in the Dalian plastination projects under Bo's supervision. In one report, Wang is quoted as saying that "to see someone executed and within minutes to see the transformation in which this person's life was extended in the bodies of several other people—it was soul-stirring."[6]

Stanford University senior research scholar Chenggang Xu offers a useful insight into how such horrors can develop within China's system. In his book *Institutional Genes*, he explains that the CCP refined the Soviet model by decentralizing the mechanics of repression, something he explained to me in detail.[7] Instead of issuing detailed orders from the top, Beijing sets broad strategic goals, then allows provinces and local officials to compete in showing how effectively they can implement them. The result is a kind of perverse market incentive, a quasi-capitalist race to achieve communist objectives.

All it takes is someone like Bo Xilai—ambitious, opportunistic, and devoid of conscience—to interpret those directives creatively. In his case, the Party's twin goals were clear: expand China's transplant industry and eradicate Falun Gong. To Bo and his psychopathic police chief, that was a win-win.

For the Chinese elite, the value was immense: on-demand organs, effectively forever. And for the Party, Falun Gong practitioners provided an abundant, expendable supply. Bo Xilai and Wang Lijun did not have to believe deeply that the Falun Gong were evil, nor did they have to see them as a particular threat. They were simply the first to figure out a way to effectively instrumentalize their eradication for the good of the party.

For several years—at least five—the practitioners regarded Jiang Zemin's campaign as a tragic mistake by the Communist Party. They said, "We're not against you. You're wrong about us. We're not what you say we are. This is propaganda. You're being misled. Please correct it."

They saw themselves as good, honest people who practiced truthfulness, compassion, and forbearance, and who, far from opposing the Party, simply wanted to be left in peace.

But in demonizing them, the Party inadvertently created a massive peaceful civil disobedience movement. Before 1999, when arrests took place in one province, groups of practitioners would travel there to appeal: "Why did you arrest these good people? You've made a mistake." Others went directly to Beijing—to Tiananmen Square, the traditional site where Chinese citizens voiced grievances against their leaders. That's what they were doing: appealing, not rebelling.

Yet despite the full weight of the state, Falun Gong has proven remarkably resistant to eradication.

That resilience cuts to the heart of what the Chinese Communist Party most fears. Totalitarianism seeks control over everything—first over property, then over the body, and finally over the soul. But practicing Falun Gong is an act that can only come from within. It cannot be imposed, and in that self-directed spiritual freedom lies the most serious threat to any totalitarian system: independent thought.

As James Madison wrote, "Conscience is the most sacred of all property." Communism seeks to abolish all private property, giving the state control over every resource and every aspect of life. The final property it strives to own is human conscience.

The CCP may seize land, wealth, and even body parts, but it has struggled mightily, and failed, to conquer the conscience of Falun Gong practitioners.

CHAPTER 5

THE EVIDENCE AND THE ROAD TO GET THERE

CHENG PEI MING: THE SURVIVOR

In August 2024, I witnessed something truly extraordinary, something I never thought I would see: a survivor of China's forced organ harvesting industry. His name is Cheng Pei Ming.

Cheng's story reads like the stuff of nightmares.

Born in 1965 in Heilongjiang Province, China, near the Russian border, Cheng led what would be called a normal existence. He was a coal miner, he was married, and he had a son. In 1998, he adopted the teachings of Falun Gong, which he states, provided him with "a meaningful life . . . [and] also benefited physical health and particularly spiritual growth."

However, in 1999, when the CCP cracked down on the Falun Gong movement, his life took a sharp turn. "Because I felt I benefited from Falun Gong," Cheng stated, "I wanted to tell the government that we are innocent, good people. So I went to protest, and I was arrested several times. A total of five times, from 1999 to 2002."[1]

It was then, in 2002, that he was sentenced to eight years in prison, according to *China Daily*, for "using a heretical religion to undermine law enforcement." During his sentence, he was tortured severely, often to the point of losing consciousness, and subjected to forced blood tests—an indicator they were considering him for organ harvesting. The torture, however, was not only physical but mental as well. "Mentally they put me and my family members under pressure as they wanted me to give up my faith in Falun Gong and if I didn't they would force my wife to divorce me when I was in prison," Cheng told *The Diplomat*.[2]

On November 16, 2004, while he was being held in a prison in northeastern China, six prison guards pinned him down in a Chinese hospital to administer anesthesia against his will. When he woke up three days later, his right foot was shackled to a hospital bed. One arm was receiving intravenous therapy, and there were tubes on his feet and chest, and into his nose.

He began coughing nonstop and felt pain and numbness around his left ribs.

Cheng, who was sentenced to an eight-year term because of his faith, was held at the Daqing Prison in Harbin, capital of Heilongjiang Province, at the time of the nonconsensual surgery.

Over the next two years, while still detained, he suffered from shortness of breath. In February 2006, he began a hunger strike in protest of a new round of torture inflicted upon him, according to reports on Minghui.org, a website dedicated to tracking firsthand accounts of the persecution. The prison administered intravenous drips and took him to Daqing Longnan Hospital on March 2, 2006, shackling him, yet again, to a bedpost.

Weak and under constant watch, Cheng heard the prison guards speaking to his sister, who had come to see him. The guards claimed that Cheng had ingested a knife blade and required a high-risk surgery. Later, a white-clad doctor came and pressed on his chest and abdomen, declaring they'd perform surgery on him the next day.

Cheng thought that would be the end of him. But an opportunity presented itself when, in the early hours of the morning, the two exhausted guards monitoring him fell asleep before putting shackles on him. He was then able to flee through a fire escape.

That was only days before Cheng read about the forced organ harvesting issue on Minghui.org. He "trembled all over" at the thought of what could have happened to him, he told me, when we spoke. He dared not take off his clothes to sleep for the next two months, just in case he had to flee.

Chinese police put out a bounty of 50,000 yuan, about $6,500 at the time, to hunt Cheng down. He lived in hiding until eventually escaping to Thailand in 2015.

It was only after escaping to the United States in 2020 and undergoing a series of medical tests that he confirmed his worst fears: Part of his liver was gone, along with a portion of his lung.

He still carries a scar, about fourteen inches long, around the left side of his chest. And to this day, his left arm and ribs ache on rainy days and when he's tired, he said.

"I'm just incredibly lucky to have survived," he told *The Epoch Times*.[3]

"Most victims of forced organ harvesting can't talk, because they're dead," Robert Destro, a former Assistant Secretary of State for Democracy, Human Rights, and Labor who facilitated Cheng's rescue to the United States, told me.

It's unclear why Cheng's abusers only partially removed his organs and allowed him to survive. Distinguished Professor Wendy Rogers, advisory board chair of the International Coalition to End Transplant Abuse in China (ETAC), offered one explanation, noting that such liver tissue could have been given to a child patient, while David Matas suggested the hospital could have been experimenting or training doctors in the craft—the initial step of a hospital getting into a business that yields massive profits, he told me.[4]

The location of the incision was also unusual: Instead of an abdominal cut typical in an organ transplant surgery, the doctors opted to make a cut between his ribs. Such a move, while uncommon, allowed wider access to organs in both the chest and abdomen.

But ultimately, "It's really up to the Chinese government or the hospital to explain what they were doing," says Matas.

Even among crimes against humanity, forced organ harvesting from prisoners of conscience is an extreme case. It's hard for people to make space in their minds for something so horrific, let alone to accept it is actually happening. Most don't want to know. Or rather, they want to know, but they also don't want to know. I've seen that conflict play out countless times, and I can't blame anyone for it. The reality is traumatic even to contemplate.

But Cheng Pei Ming changed the game.

Having followed this issue for nearly twenty years, Cheng's disclosures precipitated some unexpectedly excellent media coverage, and a substantively increased willingness among the general public to accept that it might actually be true.

Suddenly, the story was being covered as though it were just another legitimate subject for reporting—something else I'd never seen before. It's not that the issue has gone unacknowledged; it's that it's been nearly impossible to generate sustained attention or action—partly for the very reason that it's so hard to face.

Katrina Lantos Swett, president of the Lantos Foundation for Human Rights and Justice, commended Cheng's courage to speak out. She said her organization had spoken to Cheng previously and that she found his account "deeply disturbing." It offered, in her words, "further evidence of the egregious human rights abuse happening in China in the form of forced organ harvesting."[5]

Eric Patterson, the head of the Victims of Communism Memorial Foundation, similarly said the case highlighted the "urgent need to address medical atrocities carried out by the Chinese Communist Party."[6]

At an event held to tell his story, Cheng said he wasn't speaking just for himself, but for the many who are still at risk in China. He said that while detained, he and several fellow Falun Gong practitioners made each other a promise: Whoever among them made it out alive would tell the world what had happened there.

Though Cheng's efforts to make his story known are commendable and courageous and truly eye-opening regarding the crimes against humanity taking place against Chinese prisoners of conscience, "ultimately," Matas states, "the onus does not fall on Cheng to say what happened to him. The onus falls on the government of China."[7] Amazingly, perhaps because of the international attention Cheng's case was getting, several CCP propaganda media and police bureaus published a rare statement attacking him, inadvertently admitting to the regime having operated on Cheng against his will.[8] Typically, though, as we know, the Chinese government does not admit to its crimes. That is why the evidence must be made widely public and shown around the world so that these horrible acts cannot and will not go unnoticed or unpunished.

THE EVIDENCE

Cheng Pei Ming's testimony is only the latest addition to a growing body of evidence compiled over the past two decades. What follows is a chronological summary of that evidence. This summary isn't exhaustive; I'm mainly trying to offer some key revelations, and a sense of the trajectory over which the evidence base was developed. Not all entries are equivalent in importance. We'll start *before* the CCP started to persecute Falun Gong practitioners, before it created the conditions where the scale of forced organ harvesting could go full-industrial:

1984: Regulations on Organ Procurement

The CCP establishes "provisional" rules that permit the removal of organs from executed prisoners without prior consent, creating the legal framework for state-sanctioned harvesting from death-row inmates.

1994: First Documented Cases

Early human rights-related reports of organ extraction from executed Uyghur political prisoners in Xinjiang appear, later corroborated by surgeon Enver Tohti, who testified to participating in live organ removals. Human Rights Watch outlines three key findings in a 1994 report: The CCP has been using political offenders and non-violent criminals as organ donors; doctors assist in conducting pre-execution medical exams to match prisoners' organs with the needs of recipients; and prisoners' executions are often, in essence, intentionally botched so that prisoners are still alive at the time their organs are extracted.[9]

November 2005: The Lavee Anecdote[10]

Jacob Lavee talks to his patient in a Tel Aviv hospital, and the patient mentions that his insurance company has lined up a heart transplant in China in two weeks—and then the patient goes to China, gets the transplant as scheduled, and returns home. This moment (though not immediately publicized) sparks early attention from the medical community in Israel and worldwide, and plays a central role in passing Israel's 2008 law, which, among other things, bars Israeli state insurance from paying for transplants in China.

March 2006: Witness Reveals Horrors of Sujiatun Concentration Camp

An anonymous witness known as "Annie" (see chapter 1), the ex-wife of a neurosurgeon at Sujiatun Thrombosis Hospital, shares details about an underground facility that holds thousands of Falun Gong practitioners just for organ extraction.[11] According to Annie, the detainees go through medical checks like blood tests and ultrasounds to see if their organs are suitable, and they get just enough food to keep them viable. Teams of surgeons remove corneas, kidneys, livers, and skin from people who are still alive, and then the bodies are incinerated. (Later corroboration confirms that at its height, the facility held up to six thousand people.) Another account from a veteran military doctor in the Shenyang area backs this up, saying Sujiatun is one of thirty-six similar camps across China where harvesting and cremation of Falun Gong practitioners happens regularly. He explains that families of executed prisoners often get fake ashes from animals or something else, while the real bodies go to factories as materials. In early 2005, Sujiatun had over ten thousand detainees, later down to 600-750, with quick transfers using freight trains; the biggest camp in Jilin, called 672-S, holds over 120,000, treating practitioners like economic assets without reporting up the chain.

May 2006: China Forced Organ Harvesting Discussed at Auschwitz Forum[12]

I help organize and report on a press conference at the Auschwitz Center for Dialogue and Prayer; detailing reports of organ harvesting in Chinese detention facilities targeting Falun Gong practitioners. "The numbers just don't add up": The discussion highlights and unexplained organ bank is the only way to account for the massive discrepancy between China's execution and transplant numbers. A petition with over ten thousand signatures from Jewish communities calls for worldwide investigation, viewing these practices as a form of modern genocide that brings in money for military hospitals.

June 2006: Kilgour-Matas Report[13]

David Kilgour and David Matas publish a report including eighteen lines of evidence that point to widespread organ harvesting from Falun Gong practitioners. This includes an over 300 percent jump in transplants after the CCP's 1999 suppression of the group, which doesn't line up with known executions or donations. Recordings from calls to hospitals confirm organs from Falun Gong people described as healthy, with wait times of just one to two weeks compared to much longer timelines in ethical scenarios. CCP policies label Falun Gong a "heretical religion" in an effort to dehumanize them, allowing any means to be used against them, setting up a framework for forced organ harvesting. People who escaped detention describe being blood tested as a way to prepare for organ matching. The report looks at financial incentives, with big revenues for military hospitals from selling organs like kidneys for $60,000 and livers for $130,000. It notes no clear donor registry or outside checks. The authors see this as crimes against humanity and suggest stopping the use of organs from prisoners.

November 2006: Horrific New Evidence of China Organ Harvesting Revealed[14]

David Kilgour discusses China's forced organ harvesting at a Warsaw human rights forum, and tells me about how a Chinese military surgeon killed eight prisoners of conscience to supply one foreign patient with a matching kidney. The surgeon, who later quit in remorse, rejects the first seven kidneys, ostensibly from seven different individuals who were killed to procure them, as mismatches, finally accepting the eighth—something impossible in an ethical transplantation system.

2009: *Larry's Kidney* Book[15]

Daniel Asa Rose publishes a memoir, shockingly titled *Larry's Kidney: Being the True Story of How I Found Myself in China with My Black Sheep Cousin and His Mail-Order Bride, Skirting the Law to Get Him a Transplant—and Save His Life.* The book details Rose's efforts to help his cousin Larry obtain a kidney transplant in China through informal brokers who explicitly describe donors as executed prisoners, with organs becoming available in unusually short periods (often days or weeks, raising implicit suspicions of on-demand sourcing). It includes accounts of military facilitation in the process, cash-based transactions to evade records, and Rose's reflections on ethical dilemmas, including concerns that donors might encompass political prisoners or other non-consensual sources beyond common criminals.

2009: *Bloody Harvest* Book[16]

Kilgour and Matas build on their earlier work with fifty-two pieces of evidence, estimating at least forty thousand unexplained transplants from 2000 to 2005 connected to Falun Gong. They bring in United Nations reports on deaths in custody, plus discrepancies in financial data surrounding China's transplant industry that suggests non-voluntary donors. Stories from Taiwanese recipients include surgeons' notes on the good quality of organs from Falun Gong practitioners. The book examines CCP messages that reduce concern about the group. Sites that price organs highlight quick waits and reliability, with centers located in areas with many Falun Gong arrests. It covers testing of drugs on organs from prisoners, and the appeal to the CCP of the UN Special Rapporteur on Torture Manfred Nowak (and other UN officials) to explain organ harvesting evidence and resultant flimsy official denials.

2012: *State Organs* Book[17]

Edited by David Matas and Torsten Trey, this set of essays from experts looks at transplant abuses in China, focusing on Falun Gong as the key group affected, based on interviews, data, and policy breakdowns that confirm thousands of cases. Matas and Trey's opening discusses what this means for medical ethics around the world, recommending no partnerships with Chinese institutions. Ethan Gutmann's part gives estimates of sixty thousand Falun Gong deaths, backed by statements from refugees and looks into detention sites. Jacob Lavee shares his 2005 experience with a patient and how it led to changes in Israeli policy. The essays address how organ supplies from prisoners and dissidents affect research, and call for staying away from medical meetings in China. Legal and medical parts critique Western roles in trials using those organs and propose worldwide bans on transplant tourism. The accounts describe conditions in detention, required exams, and extractions, linking CCP incarceration to organ supply.

2014: *The Slaughter* Book[18]

Ethan Gutmann's book *The Slaughter* draws on 120 interviews with refugees, medical staff, and officials to estimate sixty-five thousand Falun Gong deaths for organs from 2000 to 2008, laying out how the CCP's persecution of Falun Gong practitioners grew since 1999. It tracks the massive growth of the Chinese transplant industry immediately after the persecution begins. Gutmann documents injections to mimic brain death for the extraction of organs, with the bodies being burned afterward. Investigations and escapee testimonials show the CCP's 610 Office, created specifically to enact the persecution of Falun Gong, handling the details. The book introduces Uyghurs as an early organ harvesting victim group, before the system grows to an industrial scale on the backs of Falun Gong practitioners. It's also a details credible attempts to explain the historical context and the "why" of the Falun Gong persecution, and shows preliminary information that Uyghurs are becoming a second mass victim group of the CCP's forced organ harvesting, along with possible other targeted groups like Tibetans and House Church Christians.

February 2016: Investigative Report on Tianjin First Central Hospital[19]

The powerful *Epoch Times* exposé by Matthew Robertson into Tianjin First Central Hospital, a "hospital built for murder," is a case study of how the system works. The hospital grew to five hundred beds for transplants after 1999, matching the Falun Gong persecution timing, with over five thousand procedures a year that go beyond reported donors. It highlights Tianjin's instances of "emergency transplants" where the hospital has multiple donor hearts available almost immediately for VIP patients, implying a system with backups in place, plus dedicated zones for high-profile patients sourcing organs directly from prisoners. It highlights multiple data trends that don't fit with voluntary systems, and connects to Bo Xilai's work in Liaoning.

June 2016: *Bloody Harvest/The Slaughter* Update[20]

Kilgour, Matas, and Gutmann's updated version brings in new hospital records, interviews, and numbers, projecting 60,000-100,000 transplants each year since 2000 for more than a million total, going well past official numbers. Hospital websites, which were subsequently scrubbed of incriminating content, advertise extraordinarily high transplant volumes and remarkably short wait times for organs, casting serious doubt on the effectiveness and sincerity of China's 2015 reforms that purportedly ended the use of prisoner-sourced organs. Call records have staff admitting Falun Gong and Uyghur sources, while required blood tests in prisons indicate a database for "donor" selection.

Accounts include moving fresh organs and detainees going missing, with military institutions making large incomes. Evidence from Xinjiang looks more and more like what was done to Falun Gong; statistical analysis shows that organ donation data were falsified, showing that the CCP is covering up the reality of forced organ harvesting from prisoners of conscience as they are adding a new group of victims—the Uyghurs—to be instrumentalized.

2017: Korean Chosun TV Hidden Camera Exposé[21]

A South Korean TV crew from Chosun goes undercover, posing as medical facilitators for a fictional patient needing a kidney, and sneaks into Tianjin First Central Hospital with hidden cameras. They catch doctors and brokers offering organs from "healthy" Falun Gong practitioners available in just weeks, at prices over $100,000, chatting casually about young, fresh donors that imply killing on demand rather than voluntary giving. Mobile harvesting vans parked near detention centers come up as a way to get organs fast, and the staff gives priority to foreign patients like Koreans in this "transplant tourism" setup. This footage, aired in a fifty-minute segment called "Killing to Live," shows the black market thriving despite China's 2015 claim to ban prisoner organs, exposing the reforms as a sham in a system where lives get traded openly for profit.

2018: COHRC Update on Organ Harvesting[22]

The China Organ Harvest Research Center establishes that actual annual China transplant volumes are an order of magnitude higher than official 10,000–15,000 figures, with 164 approved hospitals having minimum capacity for over 70,000 procedures per year based on government bed requirements, and many exceeding these with 100–200 percent utilization rates. While Falun Gong practitioners remain the primary victims, this report documents emerging evidence for Uyghurs (mass DNA collection in Xinjiang since 2017), adds more color on Tibetans and

House Church Christians as possible additional sources. Satellite images capture the unsettling expansion of crematoria facilities positioned directly adjacent to hospitals, hinting at a calculated increase in capacity for rapid body disposal amid rising transplant activities.

March 1, 2020: China Tribunal Judgment[23]

Under Sir Geoffrey Nice KC, a year-long, comprehensive review of the evidence on CCP forced organ harvesting, in the form of an independent people's tribunal, finds beyond a reasonable doubt that it's happening at scale and amounts to crimes against humanity: "The Tribunal's members are certain—unanimously, and sure beyond reasonable doubt—that in China forced organ harvesting from prisoners of conscience has been practiced for a substantial period of time involving a very substantial number of victims."[24]

"Falun Gong practitioners have been one—and probably the main—source of organ supply."

(The China Tribunal was initiated by, but had "scrupulous" independence from, the International Coalition to End Transplant Abuse in China (ETAC), an international nonprofit "coalition of lawyers, academics, ethicists, medical professionals, researchers, and human rights advocates dedicated to ending forced organ harvesting (a form of organ trafficking) in China" based in Australia.)[25]

Over fifty witnesses testified, including experts and investigators, along with Falun Gong practitioners who described experiences of torture, blood, ultrasound, and X-ray testing for matching, as well as people disappearing. Uyghur testimonies described forced organ scans in detention, big internments, torture, forced drugs, and DNA collection from millions in Xinjiang since 2017: "The concerted persecution and medical testing of the Uyghurs is more recent and it may be that evidence of forced organ harvesting of this group may emerge in due course."

New York Times reporter Didi Kirsten Tatlow testifies that she heard prominent Chinese surgeons discussing the use of prisoners of conscience as an organ source, demonstrating how widespread and accepted this practice had become within China, even though China states it ended this in 2015. After sharing her results with *New York Times* editors, they label such assertions "fringe" and effectively close down her investigations. Dr. Huige Li lists four ways of extraction under faked brain death. A statistical analysis, independently reviewed by a leading UK statistician, shows manipulated Chinese donation figures that do not represent the real numbers. Independent analysis of World Organization to Investigate Persecution of Falun Gong (WOIPFG) phone recordings confirm that doctors and officials admitted to extremely short waiting times for organs and that Falun Gong organs were also available.

The Tribunal rejects arguments that favor China: endorsements of the reforms by The Transplantation Society (TTS) and the World Health Organization (WHO) lack any substantial supporting evidence; positions taken by the UK and Australian governments are similarly without a solid evidential foundation; and the 2015 "reforms" (which claimed to end the use of prisoner organs) appear superficial, as indicated by persistent short wait times for transplants and ongoing expansions of hospital facilities. China's answers change from admitting use of prisoners for organs to saying they've stopped, without giving meaningful proof, even when asked.

March 10, 2020: Organ Procurement and Extrajudicial Execution[26]

The Victims of Communism Foundation's report dives into how China disguises extrajudicial killings as routine medical procedures in its organ transplant system, like when doctors declare Falun Gong practitioners "brain-dead" too soon—sometimes while they're still responsive—just to justify removing their organs while they're alive or nearly so. Chinese regulations make this easier by allowing organ extractions without needing family consent if the body goes "unclaimed" after execution or death in custody, essentially giving hospitals free rein. In Xinjiang, widespread DNA collection from millions of Uyghurs since 2016 creates a massive database that helps match and select donors based on genetic compatibility for transplants. The report calls for US actions like banning American medical training for Chinese surgeons involved in these practices, imposing sanctions on implicated hospitals and officials, and restricting any collaborations that could support China's transplant industry.

August 2020: Four Hearts in Ten Days

An *Epoch Times* story tells of a twenty-four-year-old patient named Sun Lingling, who is on life support for nine months and ends up getting four heart transplants in just ten days—from April 7 to April 16, 2020—at a Wuhan hospital tied to Huazhong University of Science and Technology. This kind of rapid availability points to an "on-demand" organ bank, where supplies seem kept ready through targeted sourcing from unwilling donors. Hospital records and expert opinions, like those from Dr. Torsten Trey and Dist. Prof. Wendy Rogers, link this to executions timed to match patient needs, with more detentions during COVID times possibly boosting the pool of potential donors. The same surgeon also does a double lung transplant on February 29 for a fifty-nine-year-old, flying in organs from hundreds of miles away from a supposed "brain-dead" donor, showing how the system handles quick, complex cases even amid a pandemic.

June 2021: 12 United Nations Special Rapporteurs and Human Rights Experts Weigh In[27]

"UN human rights experts said today they were extremely alarmed by reports of alleged 'organ harvesting' targeting minorities, including Falun Gong practitioners, Uyghurs, Tibetans, Muslims and Christians, in detention in China," stated a press release on the Office of the United Nations High Commissioner for Human Rights (OHCHR) website.[28] "The experts call on China to promptly respond to the allegations of 'organ harvesting' and to allow independent monitoring by international human rights mechanisms."[29] The statement was issued to alert the public to a joint correspondence the twelve UN Special Rapporteurs and human rights experts had sent to the Chinese government.

Susie Hughes, the cofounder and executive director of ETAC, appropriately noted, especially given the high levels of influence the CCP has at the UN: "This is such an important move by the UN HRC Special Procedures experts, and the fact they've done it speaks volumes for the credibility of the evidence at hand," and then again weighed in on the Chinese Government's response, on its predictable attacks on the witnesses, on its denials and obfuscations: "Once again Chinese officials have failed to provide official statistics on transplantations, waiting times for organ allocation or sources for organs, as requested by UN experts in 2006, 2007, and now 2021. How long will the international community tolerate this lack of transparency and absolute disregard for the value of human life?"[30]

April 2022: Global Rights Compliance Legal Advisory and Policy Guidance

Global Rights Compliance (GRC) publishes a Legal Advisory Report and supplemental Policy Guidance, *Do No Harm: Mitigating Human Rights Risks when Interacting with International Medical Institutions & Professionals in Transplantation Medicine.*[31]

The publications address serious human rights risks associated with organ transplantation medicine. GRC's Legal Advisory examines evidence of illicit and unethical practices across the globe, including particular reference to the China Tribunal's findings that the CCP has committed crimes against humanity.[32] It sets out how transplant-related medical professionals, hospitals, universities, academic journals, professional associations, and related entities may incur legal responsibility for complicity in such abuses through collaboration, training, research, funding, and/or publication involving institutions linked to these practices. Drawing on international human rights law, the UN Guiding Principles for Business and Human Rights, and selected national legal frameworks, and the Advisory emphasizes the obligation of transplant-related actors to conduct robust human rights due diligence. The accompanying Policy Guidance translates this legal analysis into specific, practical steps—risk assessment, contractual safeguards, mitigation strategies, and responsible disengagement—to help transplant-related actors avoid involvement in serious violations of human rights, while upholding core ethical standards in medicine.[33]

May 2024: DAFOH Special Report[34]

Doctors Against Forced Organ Harvesting (DAFOH) puts out a report marking twenty-five years since the CCP began its persecution of Falun Gong practitioners in July 1999, pulling together recent survivor stories and evidence of how officials tweak numbers to cover up that the harvesting still goes on. They call it a "cold genocide," where victims face drawn-out torture, abuse, and organ removals over time instead of quick mass killings. The report spots a bounce-back in transplant tourism after COVID restrictions lift, with foreigners heading to China again for fast organs. It points out big gaps in donation stats that don't add up, like way more transplants than reported donors. And it urges the world to boycott Chinese medical conferences and skip training programs for their surgeons until they address where the organs really come from.

July 2024: Cheng Pei Ming, Forced Organ Harvesting Survivor, Goes Public[35]

Cheng Pei Ming, the first known survivor of China's organ harvesting program, publicly reveals that he had been subjected to forced organ harvesting while imprisoned in China for practicing Falun Gong. After surviving the removal of parts of his liver and lung without consent, Cheng eventually escaped China and chose to go public, knowing the risks to himself and his remaining family. His testimony, supported by medical records, imaging, and expert analysis (the scans were examined by two pioneering transplant surgeons), provided rare, firsthand evidence that living prisoners of conscience are being used as involuntary organ sources, transforming long-dismissed allegations into a documented human story and garnering major media attention.[36]

February 2025: Matthew Robertson Thesis[37]

Matthew Robertson's doctoral work looks at the political economy behind organ getting in China, coining the term "extractive repression" to describe how the state turns persecution into profit by harvesting organs from targeted groups. It focuses on "execution by organ procurement"—cases where surgeons remove organs in ways that directly cause the donor's death, violating the dead donor rule that requires death before vital organ extraction. He analyzes 124,770 Chinese transplant publications from 1980 to 2015 using computational text methods, identifying seventy-one papers with flawed brain death declarations, such as placing breathing tubes after surgical incisions or noting hearts still beating during examinations. These instances span fifty-six hospitals across thirty-three cities and fifteen provinces, involving

348 medical professionals, and indicate widespread abuses before 2015, when prisoners supplied about 95 percent of organs. Descriptions of donors, including prisoners of conscience, as able to walk and pre-treated with anticoagulants like heparin suggest they are prepared for scheduled killings. Machine learning and detailed reviews confirm these violations stop appearing in literature after 2014 activist exposures. The thesis argues that post-2015 reforms conceal ongoing practices through vague language and no real oversight. It examines economic incentives for hospitals to maximize transplants for profit, a "predatory biopolitics" that treats "surplus" groups like Uyghurs as exploitable resources.

Drawing on the Minghui dataset of persecution reports and victim interviews to estimate scale, Robertson's report recommends international decoupling from China's transplant system until verifiable changes occur, with all code and data shared openly on Harvard Dataverse for others to check. The thesis package includes earlier published papers like "Analysis of official deceased organ donation data casts doubt on the credibility of China's organ transplant reform" (*BMC Medical Ethics*, 2019), and "Execution by organ procurement: Breaching the dead donor rule in China" (*American Journal of Transplantation*, 2022, co-authored with Jacob Lavee).[38]

September 2025: Putin, Xi Hot Mic Moment

Russian leader Vladimir Putin and Chinese President Xi Jinping are caught on a hot microphone discussing extending human lifespan through repeated organ transplants as they walk together towards the rostrum at Tiananmen Square for a military parade. "Earlier, people rarely lived to seventy, but these days at seventy you are still a child," Xi remarks through a translator. "As biotechnology advances, human organs can be continuously transplanted, allowing us to become younger and younger, perhaps even achieve immortality," Putin replies. The comments are broadcast to a global audience before the feed is abruptly cut off.

March 2026: Ethan Gutmann on Xinjiang

Ethan Gutmann's book titled *The Xinjiang Procedure*, details organ harvesting from Uyghurs, from survivor testimonies, with a final estimate of twenty-five thousand Uyghurs and Kazakhs—at a minimum—harvested annually since 2017, adding up to over a hundred thousand total victims.[39] It covers widespread blood and DNA testing to match organs for transplants, disappearances following medical exams, and dedicated facilities inside camps for the extractions. Conversations with refugees outline torture, forced medications, and selections for "health checks" that lead to people vanishing, drawing clear links to the Falun Gong's path from persecution to systematic slaughter. Satellite data shows crematorium expansions near hospitals, along with signs of elite transplant tourism using organs from these minorities. The work projects at least two hundred thousand deaths in the camps since 2017 and recommends international sanctions and deeper investigations into the CCP's broadening operations. Gutmann wants readers to take away the sheer horror of the camps: "Anything that you thought was impossible is actually possible," he tells me. He also highlights Ko Wen-je, the former Taipei mayor now embroiled in embezzlement scandals, whom he exposed in *The Slaughter* as taking many Taiwan nationals to China for transplants, and in *The Xinjiang Procedure*, teaching advance live organ harvesting techniques to Mainland transplant surgeons.

AN ONGOING FIGHT

The evidence is overwhelming. Over the past two decades, there has been an increase in the reporting as well as an increase in the support that this issue has received. Starting in 2007, the US Commission on International Religious Freedom (USCIRF) brought light to "multiple allegations" of state-sanctioned organ harvesting from incarcerated Falun Gong practitioners, citing the Sujiatun hospital allegations, and reported that human rights organizations were calling for independent investigations into the issue.[40] In 2012, while these allegations of organ harvesting continued to surface, the USCIRF noted that the UN Special Rapporteur on Torture called for an independent investigation and that UN Committee against Torture also called on China to conduct an independent investigation.[41]

In 2015, Chinese health officials stated that organ harvesting from prisoners was to end January 1, 2015; however, the USCIRF said in 2016 that despite the promise from China to stop this practice, reports still emerged of Falun Gong practitioners being imprisoned and subjected to torture, including "psychiatric experiments and organ harvesting from executed prisoners."[42]

It was around this same time, in 2013, that House Resolution 281 in the 113th Congress of the United States of America was introduced and advanced the next year. This resolution expressed concern over China's systematic, state-sanctioned organ harvesting from prisoners of conscience, particularly Falun Gong practitioners, and called for an investigation into these practices.[43]

Over the last decade, a plethora of such legislative efforts have been put forth, many of them not becoming law but documenting US lawmakers' concern with the issue. With each new piece of evidence, and each documented report or testimony, the support for the cause continues to grow.

Now, with Cheng Pei Ming—the one and only survivor of forced organ harvesting—coming forward with his horrific story, the decades of evidence can no longer be ignored.

Currently, three major federal bills are pending in Congress that address forced organ harvesting, with particular attention to abuses linked to Falun Gong and China. The Falun Gong Protection Act (H.R. 1540) is a China-specific measure that would require the US government to identify and impose visa bans and sanctions on foreign individuals involved in involuntary organ harvesting in China, and to produce a detailed State Department report on China's transplant system and the treatment of prisoners of conscience, including Falun Gong practitioners.[44] The Falun Gong Protection Act passed the House in May 2025 and is now awaiting consideration in the Senate Foreign Relations Committee. Its Senate companion, the Falun Gong Protection Act (S. 817), contains similar provisions focused on sanctions, reporting, and formal recognition of persecution connected to forced organ harvesting, but it has only been introduced in the Senate and likewise remains in the Senate Foreign Relations Committee with no further action yet. Alongside these, the Stop Forced Organ Harvesting Act of 2025 (H.R. 1503) takes a broader, global approach by targeting forced organ harvesting and organ-removal trafficking worldwide, authorizing sanctions against responsible individuals and adding tools such as passport denial or revocation for certain related crimes.[45] The Stop Forced Organ Harvesting Act passed the House by an overwhelming margin in May 2025 and, like the others, is currently pending in the Senate Foreign Relations Committee, though it does not yet have a Senate companion bill. There is also a new bill, the Block Organ Transplant Purchases from China Act of 2025 (H.R. 2114, "BLOCK Act"). Being looked at by the House Foreign Affairs Committee, this bill would bar federal Medicare and Medicaid funds from covering transplants sourced in China. None of these proposals have become law, but the fight is ongoing, and stronger than ever. In December of 2025, the *Epoch Times* covered a joint DAFOH–ETAC petition, which gained over 505,000 signatures, from more than fifty countries, and advocated for G7 nations, along with several others, to implement measures to combat the CCP's forced organ harvesting practices. [46] The petition references the final conclusions reached by the China Tribunal, showing that as the evidence continues to pile up, these crimes against humanity can no longer be ignored.[47]

CHAPTER 6

WHY COMMUNIST SYSTEMS—AND THE CCP IN PARTICULAR—ENABLE FORCED ORGAN HARVESTING

THE DEVASTATING CONSEQUENCES OF MISUNDERSTANDING A TOTALITARIAN STATE

To understand China—and, ultimately, its relationship with the West—we have to look closely at how the current Chinese system is uniquely designed to enable something as monstrous as forced organ harvesting from living "donors" like Cheng Pei Ming and the hundreds of thousands of others who, unlike Cheng, did not survive. It is neither an accident nor an aberration. Rather, it is the logical outcome of a system that sustains itself through murder, terror, and the belief that any means are justified so long as they serve the Party's ends.

There are three brilliant people whom I interviewed that played a pivotal role in building my understanding of the true nature of communism—Chenggang Xu, Harrison Koehli, and John Lenczowski—each of whom offers a distinct but complementary perspective on how the system functions, and why understanding it matters. Their insights help illuminate the mechanisms of control that make such atrocities possible, and why misunderstanding the nature of the Chinese totalitarian state carries consequences that reach far beyond China's borders. I encourage you to explore their work beyond my brief exploration here.

The first thing to understand is that Chinese Communism is built on the idea of absolute, top-down control. It is not merely authoritarian; it is totalitarian in the most extreme sense of the word. Understanding the difference between authoritarian and totalitarian systems, as discussed earlier, is crucial. Under totalitarianism, there are no independent organizations of any kind. The CCP has an obsessive commitment to ensuring that none exist. This point is often misunderstood, but it is essential: the suppression of all independent organization and dissent—through violence, ideology, and fear—is central to the Party's survival.

The supremacy of the Party is absolute. Its first imperative is always to eliminate opposition and maintain control.

What Chenggang Xu has done—through twenty years of studying Chinese communism—is to explain how the Party managed to sustain totalitarian rule in China even as the Soviet Union collapsed. He calls this system "regionally administered totalitarianism," or RADT.

In such a system, the Party does not issue direct, detailed orders; instead, it sets strategic direction. Regional and local officials then compete to implement that strategy, each trying to outperform the others. At every level, superiors evaluate subordinates: "Are you being a good communist or not? Are you going to get your graft money this year, or will we cut you off because you're not expanding the organ industry fast enough, given that it's one of our priorities?"

Within that structure, all it took was for figures like Bo Xilai and Wang Lijun to see the opportunity and think, *Aha—win-win.* They could grow the transplant industry while helping to eradicate Falun Gong—through "reeducation" when possible, and through murder when not. Everyone benefited: Bo gained political capital and wealth; Party elites secured access to organs; and the system appeared to be producing results. For Bo, it was the perfect solution to multiple problems at once.

But a system like this doesn't stop there. Once others saw what Bo was doing, they recognized that his success could be replicated. They thought, *I'd better get on this train. If I don't, I'll look like the one not implementing this brilliant new Party policy.*

This is the dark genius of Chenggang Xu's model: it reveals how the Party's moral void becomes a feature, not a flaw. In a system built on regionally administered totalitarianism, evil doesn't need to be ordered from the top; it emerges organically. Each region, each bureau, each official competes to interpret the Party's wishes in the most "effective" way, often by pushing moral boundaries even further. The incentives are perverse but clear: those who display the greatest loyalty, the greatest ruthlessness, are rewarded.

The result is a self-propelling repression machine.

This leads quite organically to another essential feature of Chinese communism: the Party is a pathocracy, a system in which psychopaths (or people we would describe today as having Cluster B or dark triad personalities) rise to the top. Communist totalitarianism is deeply linked to psychopathology. Whether this is by design or a secondary effect of the perverse incentive structures inherent to communism is an interesting question. What's clear is that by infiltrating and dominating society, a "pathocracy" of systemic evil is forged through a process called "ponerization." Harrison Koehli, who today holds Andrzej Łobaczewski's brain trust, described it to me as "the process by which increasingly psychopathic individuals infiltrate a group, take over the leadership positions, become more inspirational and influential within the system, and have a deforming effect on the group itself and the group's ideology." According to Koehli, that is what happens first at a local, and then at a societal level in communist systems. It must be stressed that we are not talking about all Chinese people, but rather a very small but powerful subset of society. In a ponerized society, some citizens, through their resilience, cultural depth, and faith, manage to preserve or recover their moral compass even while living under a system that relentlessly promotes nihilism from the top down. Others, the majority, adjust to the new normal via "psychological adaptations that help with life in pathocracy for various reasons, but are fundamentally unhealthy," such as tendencies for inordinate deception and secrecy, Koehli tells me.

Which brings us to the third thing to understand: for communism to be operational, you don't need people to believe in it. You only need them to pretend to believe in it. John Lenczowski, who served as President Reagan's chief Soviet affairs advisor on the National Security Council and later founded the Institute of World Politics in Washington, DC, has written widely on this topic. He once explained that it's a mistake to think a country stops being communist simply because its people no longer believe in communism.

You hear this about China all the time—that it's "capitalist now," that people are allowed to get rich and pursue personal wealth. And that's true to a degree. "To be rich is glorious," Deng Xiaoping famously said as the Party sought to pull China out of economic collapse. Allowing limited prosperity was a survival tactic, not an ideological shift.

As Lenczowski puts it, what matters is not belief but operation. The question isn't whether people believe in communism, but whether communism is operational.

Václav Havel illustrated this idea through the story of the greengrocer in his landmark essay, "The Power of the Powerless." The grocer hangs a sign in his shop window that reads, "Workers of the world, unite." He doesn't care about workers uniting; he hangs the sign to signal compliance. It tells the authorities, and his neighbors, that he won't make trouble. He'll be left alone. It doesn't matter whether he believes in the slogan. What matters is that he obeys, and that the system continues to function.

In fact, it may even be better for the system if people don't believe. When you act against your conscience, when you perform loyalty to something you know is false, you compromise yourself. Each act of obedience corrodes your moral strength a little more. Over time, that erosion makes resistance almost impossible.

Ultimately, the only thing that matters is whether the Communist Party remains the supreme force in society. That—not belief, not prosperity—is what defines a communist system.

HOW A FORCED ORGAN HARVESTING INDUSTRY THRIVES UNDER CCP CONDITIONS

Nevertheless, while the conditions in communist China make such crimes against humanity *possible*, a mass forced organ-harvesting system on the scale the CCP built does not appear overnight. It requires years of deliberate policy, coordinated effort, and an intentional campaign to make it operational.

First, a kind of ideological conditioning is an essential prerequisite for any crime at the level of a crime against humanity: most people are not psychopaths, and will not willingly accept the mass killing or destruction of an entire group unless they have first been taught to see that group as less than human.

So the system must systematically dehumanize a large population through propaganda, much as the Nazis did to the Jews in the 1930s.

The next requirement—and logical step—is the mass incarceration of that population, making them a large captive group with no rights and no visibility. In such conditions, detainees become especially vulnerable: as people are routinely tortured, transferred, or moved between prisons, labor camps, *laogai*, and black sites, and because many refused to give their names (to avoid reprisals against their families), individuals simply "disappeared" on a daily basis. They might have been released, moved, or tortured to death—there is no way for the other prisoners to know. (Interviews with Falun Gong dissidents describe the sound of fellow practitioners screaming under torture in these facilities.)

Once you have this incarcerated population, the next step is to build a database of potential "donors."

Social data scientist Matthew Robertson, former *Epoch Times* investigative journalist and now Victims of Communism Memorial Foundation senior fellow, as well as one of the top researchers on China forced organ harvesting has reported that Detained Falun Gong practitioners were subjected to systematic blood tests, urine samples, ultrasounds, X-rays, and CT scans targeting organs—assessments conducted not for health care but for organ compatibility and viability. More recently, after the CCP incarcerated over a million Uyghurs, they too were subjected to coercive DNA collection, blood typing, urine testing, ultrasounds, and ECGs under mass-surveillance programs, with biometric data used to enable tissue matching for transplantation.[1]

Finally, if you are one of China's roughly seven million "red card" holders with privileged access to all levels of the medical system, all you need is a doctor's recommendation for a transplant, and you instantly have access to a ready "farm" of organs.

In the early years, hospitals even advertised these services openly (a practice that diminished after 2006, after Jacob Lavee and "Annie" came forward), and later they promoted them more discreetly. Once a patient submits their medical data, the People's

Liberation Army's logistics network can locate a compatible detainee, transport them to the hospital that arranged the transplant, and carry out a kill-to-order procedure.

From there, the evil only expands. A disturbing new investigative report reveals that China's forced organ harvesting, which on the backs of Falun Gong practitioners grew exponentially from a relatively small operation focused on Death Row prisoners, Uyghurs, and other undesirables, and later added Uyghurs as a second large-scale victim group, has further expanded in horrifying ways.[2]

Evidence now points to the deliberate "farming" of babies, through state-linked surrogacy programs and the seizure of infants born to detained mothers, specifically to harvest their organs while still alive. Some wealthy but morally compromised can have a child through surrogacy, and then use that child as a highly effective "donor," with a 50 percent shared genome—surgical techniques and physiological adaptations make this feasible with good outcomes.

I was recently asked on a Doctors Against Forced Organ Harvesting (DAFOH)-organized panel what I thought of these reports. DAFOH was the first organization, founded in 2006 by Dr. Torsten Trey, to form around researching and exposing forced organ harvesting. It was also "chartered as a contribution to mankind to protect ethical medical practices that further human dignity."[3] I replied that while I've become somewhat desensitized to the issue of forced organ harvesting, having been speaking about it for almost twenty years, it took me several days to bring myself to read the reports in detail. That same horror I experienced back in 2006, that desire not to believe, not know, had come back. I saw immediately that the perverse incentive structures all aligned in the same direction: that this was almost certainly happening, and the evidence was compelling. Sir Geoffrey Nice KC, who chaired the China Tribunal back in 2018–2020, was also on the panel, and responded to me, in his trademark measured, logical fashion:

> The improbability or unbelievability argument is actually very easy to deal with, and I'm surprised that people don't deploy the argument swiftly. There was already a system applied to capital punishment—Death Row prisoners—and all that had to be done was to open another door of the prison into an existing system where all the people needed to operate the system were in place. It's rather similar to what might have happened in the gas chambers operated in Nazi Germany if yet another category of people had been subject to what was being done, mostly to Jews, but also to other people. Opening another door to an existing system is not unbelievable at all. And so, although I sympathize with those who found it very difficult to read about and to accept that these things were happening, actually, it's very obvious that they could, as well as evidence-based that they did.

The next new door that has been opened is this: Military hospitals are implicated in removing hearts, livers, and kidneys from newborns and premature infants, often within hours of demand. Whistleblowers describe a systematic pipeline supplying pediatric organs to elite Party members and wealthy clients.[4]

Meanwhile, the world stands idly by for years and allows the Falun Gong persecution to happen, allows the organ harvesting industry to grow unchecked, and then spread its wings further by adding Uyghurs to its deathly fodder. And now this.

As the persecution intensified, and Falun Gong practitioners went more and more underground, practitioners learned ways to truth-tell under CCP duress. But the media, even today, remains largely uninterested.

That wasn't always the case. At the beginning of Jiang's campaign of persecution of Falun Gong, Western media outlets were largely sympathetic in their coverage of Falun Gong. That all changed with a 2001 *New York Times* interview.

On August 8, 2001, *New York Times* publisher Arthur Sulzberger Jr. led a high-profile delegation—including executive editor Joseph Lelyveld, incoming editor Howell Raines, columnist Thomas L. Friedman, and several Beijing correspondents—into the Zhongnanhai leadership compound for a rare, hour-long interview with Chinese President Jiang Zemin.

The meeting occurred at the height of the CCP's intensifying attack on Falun Gong, which Jiang had personally ordered two years earlier in July 1999 when he labeled the practice an "evil cult" and vowed to "eliminate [it] in three months." With the movement proving far more resilient than Jiang anticipated, the interview offered him a powerful stage to influence one of the world's most influential newspapers and shape Western understanding of the campaign he had launched.

In the interview, Jiang used the *Times* as a direct conduit to portray Falun Gong in the harshest possible terms, describing it as a movement that encouraged "suicide" and "self-immolation" and depicting it as a destabilizing "heretical organization." These claims functioned as a political defense of his crackdown, yet instead of contextualizing or challenging them, the *Times* reproduced his remarks largely unfiltered.

This moment marked a turning point. Until then, Western coverage had generally been more balanced and sympathetic, highlighting Falun Gong's roots as a qigong-based moral practice centered on Truthfulness, Compassion, and Forbearance, and portraying the state's reaction as excessive. In 1999, for example, *The New York Times* described a gathering of ten thousand practitioners near Zhongnanhai as a peaceful sit-in by "qigong enthusiasts." The *Wall Street Journal* went even further: Ian Johnson's

Pulitzer-winning reporting humanized practitioners and exposed wrongful detentions, including the case of a woman whose mother died in police custody. The *Washington Post* likewise treated Falun Gong as a broad "health craze" caught in authoritarian overreach, while outlets like the BBC and CNN characterized it as a "fast-growing spiritual movement" rather than a danger to society.

After the Sulzberger interview, however, coverage across major outlets began to echo the Party's framing, increasingly referring to Falun Gong as a "cult" or "sect" and implicitly endorsing the idea that it posed a threat. Jiang exploited his unprecedented access to rail against the group for nearly twenty minutes, boasting that the state had "reformed" 90 percent of practitioners through "education"—a euphemism for coercive re-education camps. The *Times* amplified these talking points verbatim, and Jiang even praised the newspaper as "a very good paper," a comment that critics later interpreted as evidence of the mutual incentives at play.

Analysts, including investigative work later highlighted by *Epoch Times* reporting, have argued that this interview marked a decisive shift: by 2001, coverage increasingly parroted Beijing's cult rhetoric without offering robust rebuttal, even after the *Washington Post* debunked key CCP claims such as the staged "self-immolation" incident.

In the years following the interview, this reframing hardened into a new media default. Between 2001 and 2005, prominent *Times* pieces repeated Jiang's "cult" characterization while marginalizing practitioner testimony. Other outlets followed suit: BBC reports began referring to the group as a "banned cult"; and the *Guardian* emphasized supposed "extremism" despite the absence of any violent record.

The consequences were significant. As Western media grew more skeptical or dismissive, Beijing faced less international scrutiny. Reports of forced organ harvesting that emerged in

2006 met with heightened doubt, and even high-profile lawsuits against Jiang—including a 2005 case in Argentina—received little coverage.

The Sulzberger interview exemplified the concept of "elite capture": Western media trading healthy skepticism of communist party narratives for access. The interview did not single-handedly transform coverage, but it amplified an emerging trend—shifting the portrayal of Falun Gong from victims of authoritarian repression to subjects of a supposed "cult" panic, with lasting implications for global understanding of the persecution.

The CCP's organ harvesting has now gone on unchecked for more than two decades, and the CCP, unafraid of critical coverage from Western outlets, has found other convenient groups to harvest from, including the Uyghurs—these allegations even easier to deny as the Uyghurs lie predominantly in an isolated, military-controlled zone. Although thus far direct evidence of forced organ harvesting is scant, Tibetans and House Church Christians are in the CCP's crosshairs much in the way Falun Gong and Uyghurs have been, and the CCP's persecution of Christians is escalating as I write, during Christmas 2025. We also know that the CCP plans to expand its abhorrent methodology to foreigners—Taiwanese soldiers—in the event of a Taiwan invasion.

According to recent reporting in *The Epoch Times* by Eva Fu, Dr. Zheng Zhi, "a former Chinese military doctor currently living in exile in Canada, who witnessed the Chinese communist regime's forced harvesting of organs from a living person years ago, said Beijing had long made plans to take Taiwanese soldiers' blood, skin, and organs in the event of a Taiwan invasion."

> "Once a war breaks out in the Taiwan Strait, the greatest pressure for them will be on logistics support," he said. Millions of troops may be mobilized to the front line of

> the Taiwan Strait, including possibly 2 million to 3 million logistics personnel, he said.
>
> He said that from the Chinese regime's view, "the most difficult part of the logistics to supply the front is the storage, refrigeration, and transportation of blood, as many soldiers will be bleeding or burned in combat," and "blood supply will become the biggest pressure."
>
> The Chinese military solution was to put surrendered or captured Taiwanese soldiers in detention, draw their blood, and use it for wounded Chinese soldiers, according to Zheng. He said they proposed to take skin from the Taiwanese soldiers and transplant it onto the Chinese soldiers who have burns.
>
> So if the Chinese Communist Party (CCP) attacks Taiwan and the Taiwanese military surrenders, "the first thing they might face is having their blood taken because a large blood supply is needed to sustain a war," Zheng said.
>
> He said that the Chinese military has developed modular blood processing equipment for blood testing and processing. Using container trucks and airplanes, the blood could be quickly transported to the frontlines to "immediately set up a field hospital," he added.
>
> There are "no technical barriers."[5]

"Killed to order" has become so normalized in China that it's regularly written into published Chinese transplant literature.

And it has become a centerpiece of the Chinese elites' longevity program, Project 981.

Recently in *The Epoch Times*, Eva Fu and I reported how for decades, the 981 Project "was known only to Beijing's elites and a few in the West who probe the dark corners of China's no-holds-barred medical research. Studded with star physicians, the shadowy project poses as the pathway to longevity, the latest in almost a century of insider health perks for the upper echelons of the Chinese Communist Party."

> Archives of the 981 Project website show that its Beijing medical center has 11 departments, although they aren't listed individually, making it hard to gauge whether the project directly conducts transplant surgeries.
>
> Regardless, there are more than enough medical facilities in its network that can provide transplants upon referral, Trey said. The project has hundreds of partnering hospitals; many are on an international investigator's watchlist for potential abuses because of their large volumes of transplants. Among them is the 301 Hospital, formally known as Beijing's People's Liberation Army General Hospital and the source of the 2019 ad that resurfaced after Xi's remark about living to 150.
>
> The 301 Hospital is the country's largest military hospital and serves top Chinese authorities and military units.
>
> South of a garden and adjacent to a state guest building is the southern building, a closely guarded wing and the go-to place for top-ranking officials when they fall ill.
>
> The same physicians who have attended to the communist leaders are now at the 981 Project, working toward the longevity goal.
>
> In 2011, the 301 Hospital arranged a liver transplant for Wang Ying, a police bureau director who oversaw the local suppression of Falun Gong. He was lauded by the regime as an "exemplary role model," according to Chinese state media reports.
>
> The time between hospitalization and surgery was less than three months.
>
> After the surgery, Yang Huanning, the regime's deputy public security minister, paid a visit to pass along well wishes from his own bosses and said that the hospital had

> provided "first-rate technological and medical conditions" and that the "related political and legal departments" had done "every preparatory work within their means," Chinese media stated.
>
> One official overseeing Wang's operation was Zhou Yongkang, then China's third-most powerful man, whom Beijing linked to illicit organ abuses after he fell from favor.
>
> Chinese officials have on-demand access to organs when they need them, according to a source with deep knowledge of the Chinese medical system who consults with high-level Chinese officials. The individual requested anonymity out of fear of retaliation.[6]

Together, these details reveal a system designed not only to preserve the lives of China's political elite, but to do so through a vast medical apparatus built on secrecy, privilege, and coercive access to human organs. In this light, Project 981, like the forced organ harvesting industry itself, is not an aberration but the logical culmination of a Party-state that treats the bodies of its citizens as a resource to be allocated for the survival of those at the top.

A few words about Eva, my co-author in the above-referenced article, who did much of the heavy lifting in getting it to the finish line (I encourage you to read it in full!). Earlier in 2025 Eva won the Wilbur Award, the Religion Communicators Council (RCC)'s top honor, presented annually to recognize the most outstanding work in the communication of religious issues, values, and themes in secular media. She won for a collection of exposés titled *Killing the Faithful for Organs: The Brutal Secret Beijing Doesn't Want Exposed*, alongside other 2025 Wilbur honorees from *The Associated Press*, *NPR*, *Harper's Magazine*, and CBS' *60 Minutes*. Be sure to follow her work closely. She is *the* rising star in the difficult world of reporting on the Chinese communist party's greatest excesses and darkest secrets.

CHAPTER 7

MAKE EVERYONE COMPLICIT—INCLUDING YOUR ADVERSARIES

ROB, REPLICATE, AND REPLACE

As we've seen, indiscriminate persecution and murder are built into the communist system. They serve a purpose: to keep society afraid, compliant, and, most importantly, complicit. In the communist system, incentive structures are inverted. Unethical means to a desired end are always permissible, provided they don't challenge the Party's authority. The CCP has no regard for individual human life. The Chinese people belong to the state and can therefore be used as the Party sees fit. Utilitarian bioethics serves as the moral foundation of CCP medical principles. Inevitably, that worldview leads to deadly practices, such as organ harvesting, the one-child policy, and forced abortions, among others.

By design, the system also works to make everyone complicit

in its crimes, thereby eliminating any possible moral high ground. Anyone who tries to claim such ground becomes an example who is punished publicly to reinforce the lesson.

Consider what happened to Gao Zhisheng, once celebrated by the Ministry of Justice itself as one of China's top ten lawyers—a self-made man who rose from abject poverty to national prominence by winning impossible cases. Then he made one unforgivable choice: he defended Falun Gong practitioners and exposed their torture in open letters to President Hu Jintao and Premier Wen Jiabao. The Party stripped his license, arrested him in 2006, tortured him with electric batons to the genitals, cigarette burns, and toothpicks driven into his flesh. Released briefly, he refused to recant. Rearrested, tortured again, he still refused. In August 2017, he vanished completely—kidnapped from his village home by state security, never seen again in public. Gao would not bend, would not participate in the lie. So, the Party erased him. Most people, when faced with that choice, choose to live—and in choosing, they become complicit. The unjust consequences of Gao's silence scream the price of refusal.

Nowhere is the CCP's utter lack of ethics and "Party above all else" mentality more apparent than in its model of economic development—"rob, replicate, and replace." This strategy has allowed China to leapfrog the normal process of incremental growth that most developing nations must endure, while ensnaring its economic partners in a web of moral compromise that is now exceedingly difficult to escape.

Entanglement was always the goal.

Indeed, the United States' partnership with China was based on a fundamental misunderstanding of the nature of the Chinese state—its ideology, its operations, and the true nature of its goals.

The story goes that in the 1980s, one of America's most prominent bankers visited China and began discussions with senior officials. He quickly realized that many of China's state-owned enterprises were in dire financial condition, with some on the verge of collapse. This wasn't entirely surprising for a communist state like China, yet it was equally clear that these entities were, in effect, "too big to fail." They were owned by the state, which meant they were ultimately owned and controlled by the Communist Party elite. Their failure was impossible not because the financials were sound, but because the Party would never allow it.

The entire country would collapse before those businesses went under.

It occurred to this banker that he could capitalize on these Party-owned enterprises. He could return to the United States and persuade his bank, and others within the financial elite, to list these Chinese state-owned companies on the US stock exchange. In his estimation, it was as close to a guaranteed investment as one could get. The state couldn't lose.

The banker and his partners got their pitch airtight. And somehow, the SEC agreed to a special allowance for China, a reduced, minimal auditing standard for Chinese companies on US exchanges. The CCP uses the excuse of protecting "state secrets" to prevent the US Public Company Accounting Oversight Board (PCAOB) from properly auditing its companies. This created an absurd arrangement in which the equivalent of a prospectus and a few promises were considered sufficient for evaluation. Of course, there are extensive financial irregularities that have been documented over the years. On paper the CCP has recently agreed to more oversight, but it's not clear to me how seriously this is being enforced. And to this day, Chinese companies listed on US markets aren't even directly owned by the people who appear to own them. Ownership is routed through a maze of Cayman Islands contracts and other opaque structures.

Of course, the true value of these enterprises remains unknown outside of China—they are classified as state secrets. Yet hundreds of billions of dollars have been capitalized this way. It's money the banks don't really have, because the actual value is unlikely to approach the stated value. But they have to pretend otherwise, because how could they ever unwind it now?

In a way, this wasn't seen at the time as a mistake—certainly not one of epic proportions. Rather, it fit nicely with the so-called Kissinger Doctrine, which held that American engagement with China was essential: if the United States didn't enter, someone else would seize the opportunity of a billion-person market, which, of course, didn't yet exist, but seemed as though it might one day. (It was Henry Kissinger, secretary of state in the mid-1970s under presidents Richard Nixon then Gerald Ford, who first created the mania around "getting into China," his own ideas of the country based also on a series of profound misunderstandings.)

The prevailing wisdom was that engagement would *change* China—that as it integrated with the global economy, it would naturally become more democratic. That assumption, or rhetoric, guided policy for decades. It's what led the United States to grant China access to the World Trade Organization in 2001, even though China failed to meet many of the qualifying standards. It's what originally drove President Clinton to sever the link between Most Favored Nation (MFN) status and human rights in 1994. It's what pushed Congress to grant Permanent Normal Trade Relations (PNTR) in 2000. It's what kept Western leaders and CEOs almost silent when, in July 1999, just as the final WTO deal was coming together, Jiang Zemin launched the nationwide campaign against Falun Gong, rounding up millions for torture, forced labor, psychiatric abuse, and of course forced organ harvesting. Business was too important; the "historic opportunity" could not be jeopardized by mere human rights concerns.

Alongside this insistence that the Americans look the other way on corporate transparency, the Chinese made another highly calculated demand. Any American company wishing to partner with a Chinese enterprise had to agree to transfer its intellectual property to its Chinese counterpart. In every joint venture, a Chinese partner would be assigned, and technology transfer was mandatory.

The result, decades after these types of partnerships began, is that Chinese companies are now siphoning off the best and brightest of American intellectual property with impunity.

There are countless examples of China gutting American companies from the inside out. One well-known case is Segway—the self-balancing personal transport device. Segway was a somewhat successful but niche American company. It entered into a partnership with a Chinese firm, which, as part of the agreement, gained access to its IP. The Chinese partner used that technology to start a competing company, undercut Segway's prices, and eventually drove down its value to the point that they could buy it outright. That pattern has been repeated many times.

Another example is the solar industry. The Chinese government identified solar energy as a national security priority for several reasons. There was a growing mania for solar power in the United States, and China had ready access to rare earth elements—materials essential for solar panels and other advanced technologies. Rare earths aren't "rare" because they're scarce, but because they occur in low concentrations per ton of ore. Extraction is costly and environmentally damaging. But in a country with weak or easily skirted environmental regulations, it becomes cheap, and strategically useful.

By manipulating prices and flooding the global market, China drove out competitors. Today, nearly all solar panels are produced by Chinese companies. They own the market. That dominance was no accident; it was a deliberate part of their national strategy.

This pattern has repeated across sectors: steel, electronics, pharmaceuticals, and more. In every case, it's the same model—target a key industry, extract or replicate its intellectual property, and then use state power to crush competitors and capture the market. Nothing in China operates independently; every major industry functions as part of the regime's larger strategic design.

HIDE YOUR STRENGTH, BIDE YOUR TIME

At the same time that the Chinese economy was being integrated into the American financial system, Deng Xiaoping, the former Chinese leader, was pursuing his "hide your strength and bide your time" policy. The idea was that China must develop its strength quietly, without anyone knowing, and always with humility: "We're not big enough. We really need your help, America."

The duplicity is staggering. It should not be surprising that Jiang Zemin's job before he became paramount leader was, to, in so many words, "fool the barbarians." As the mayor of Beijing, he was one of the leaders who met with American businessmen, to put on this front of what China supposedly was: friendly, full of opportunity, a little rough around the edges, sure, but full of progressives trying to move things in the right direction.

"Don't upset the hardliners," he'd say, "because then we won't be able to have our cushy business deals." He was the expert at that. And that's when America really got fully in bed with China. That's part of the reason why the persecution was so hard to talk about or validate, because doing so would upset massive interests being developed by the most elite Americans, many of whom believed they were going to "change China."

A "PEOPLE'S WAR" AGAINST AMERICA

The truth is that China is, and has always been, waging a "people's war" against the United States, as the *People's Daily* openly declared in May 2019 amid the trade war escalation. It is subtle, patient, and deeply pernicious. But the evidence is all around us.

It is not difficult to make the case, for instance, that the sudden explosion of fentanyl addiction in the United States stems directly from deliberate decisions made by the Chinese regime that would weaken, divide, distract, and degrade American society.

Nothing in China happens without the Party's permission. Even organized crime operates as an arm of the Party. That point is worth underscoring, because it illustrates the principle that underlies the entire system: everything functions under the Party's auspices—even a global drug trade.

Repeatedly during the Obama administration, Xi Jinping promised to address the fentanyl problem. But nothing meaningful was done. Around that time, I heard that Chinese authorities had wiped out one of the Fujian triads (organized crime groups from China's Fujian province)—eliminated them completely, to make a statement. Our reporting and many others' reporting has shown that the CCP selectively tolerates and co-opts organized crime. Whether that particular story is literal or symbolic, the message it sent was unmistakable: the Party is the ultimate authority. Criminal organizations were free to continue their activities, so long as they paid the appropriate tribute and did not conflict with Party interests. When they did, the results were swift and final.

This dynamic reflects what Michel Juneau-Katsuya, the former Asia-Pacific Bureau Chief of the Canadian Security Intelligence Service, calls the "Unholy Trinity"—a cooperative network of the Chinese state security apparatus, powerful business tycoons, and organized crime triads, all working toward the same strategic goals.[1]

In November 2025, FBI Director Kash Patel traveled to Beijing and, armed with pressure from the full force of the United States government, secured the most specific, verifiable agreement ever extracted from the Chinese Communist Party on fentanyl. It was a commitment to fully designate, schedule, and crack down on all thirteen precursor chemicals—plus seven additional subsidiaries—used to manufacture the poison that's killed hundreds of thousands of Americans. If actually implemented, it would shut the spigot. But will the CCP actually comply?

The very specific and verifiable nature of the commitments is a new thing for the CCP, but history would tell us the answer is "no." This is the same regime that promised Hong Kong fifty years of freedom and then crushed it, that swore WTO compliance while stealing technology blind, that signed countless deals only to violate them the moment the cameras turned off—can we really expect the CCP to alter its unchanging playbook? Unless, of course, the US has privately advised the CCP that it *really is* watching closely, and that not complying with the exact terms of the agreement, overtly or covertly, will lead to significant pain. This is the only language the CCP understands. Otherwise, they'll most likely smile, pocket the tariff relief, plead bureaucratic limitations, and keep the precursors flowing through back channels. They've done it every single time before.

This all goes hand in hand with the doctrine of "hide your strength, bide your time."

Until the Trump administration began imposing tariffs and renegotiating trade terms, the CCP had not, in my view, done a single thing it didn't already want to do. Every foreign policy decision, every trade deal, every act of engagement was calculated to serve the Party's own interests, which, by definition, meant a loss for its rivals. The CCP does not believe in "win-win." For them, it's only a win if the other side loses. Or, another way to explain CCP logic is: win-win is "two wins for me."

The current strain on Xi Jinping's leadership reflects a growing belief among many Party elites that he broke with the "hide your strength, bide your time" policy too early. Perhaps the shift came as a reaction to Trump being the first American president to seriously challenge the CCP's ambitions. For two decades, the Party had grown accustomed to getting virtually everything it wanted. The prevailing attitude among the elite was: These barbarians are naïve; we have them completely in our pocket. That sense of complacent superiority became the norm.

Then, suddenly, they were forced into a situation that wasn't entirely to their advantage. And when that happened, the blame naturally fell on Xi. He was accused of upsetting the system, of revealing China's intentions too soon.

Still, once the CCP began acting openly aggressive—rather than quietly so—it became difficult for everyone involved to retreat. Take the construction of artificial islands in the South China Sea: first, they said they wouldn't build them; then they built them. Then they claimed they wouldn't militarize them; soon after, military structures appeared. It was the same pattern of incremental escalation—slow enough to avoid confrontation at each step, but cumulative enough to change the strategic reality. It's the proverbial frog boiling in water—no single act seemed alarming in isolation, but together they marked a clear escalation.

The Trump administration had noticed this escalation, and their reaction, in turn, has fueled internal tensions within the CCP. Xi's more overt posture may have been partly a response to external pressure, but it also exposed divisions inside the Party itself—a growing power struggle over how best to preserve China's dominance without jeopardizing the system that made it possible.

Internal power struggles aside, externally, the goal remains unchanged: to win the war against the free world, ideally without firing a shot. And it is working. We may recoil in horror at the thought of something as obviously evil as forced organ harvesting, but a CCP-inspired Marxist ideology is infecting, corrupting, and orally debasing Western societies at an alarming rate, and the true nature of it is going unnoticed. Which is why understanding China's organ harvesting—its anti-humanity, its total lack of ethics—provides such a window into the true nature of the CCP and the global implications of an unchecked totalitarian regime.

PART II

THE GLOBAL IMPLICATIONS OF CHINA'S FORCED ORGAN HARVESTING INDUSTRY

CHAPTER 8

ZERO SUM: HOW THE CCP PERCEIVES AMERICA

WHAT A CCP VICTORY LOOKS LIKE

Forced organ harvesting—cruel, evil, and inhuman as it is—is only one small piece of a larger puzzle of how the CCP operates and how it seeks to export its ideology abroad. A major part of that operation, in fact, lies in the Party's complex and often misunderstood relationship with the United States.

To understand that relationship, we must understand how the CCP perceives America; and to do that, we have to grasp what *victory* looks like from the Chinese Communist Party's perspective—a terrifying vision of a China-centric global order in which the CCP controls key industries, institutions, and trade networks; where totalitarianism is viewed as the winning system; and where Western-style liberal democracy is discredited, degraded, and put on the defensive.

As Michael Pillsbury, one of the world's experts on China,

outlines in his classic book *The 100-Year Marathon*, the CCP has been pursuing a long-term, covert strategy since 1949 to become the world's dominant superpower by 2049. From the Party's point of view, it is already at war with the United States, and there can be only one winner. To achieve that victory, the CCP draws on the ancient stratagems of Sun Tzu's *The Art of War*—balancing competition with cooperation, avoiding direct confrontation until it is strong enough to prevail, ideally without ever firing a shot.

A central element of that strategy is concealment: the CCP seeks to hide any actions that might provoke a global backlash, to appear cooperative, and to advance incrementally—both economically, technologically, and geopolitically. Instead of all-out kinetic war as we've thought of it in the past, the CCP hopes to "win" by exporting its morally bankrupt, totalitarian, and utilitarian system through technology, international institutional capture, and an intricate web of incentives and coercion applied across governments and industries. It does so systemically, deliberately, and aggressively—but patiently, and quietly as well.

In measuring its progress, the CCP begins by evaluating every country, especially the United States, through the lens of what Cleo Paskal, one of the world's leading experts on CCP influence operations in the Asia-Pacific, calls Comprehensive National Power. Paskal argues that the Chinese Communist Party looks at every country, every region, every sector, and asks: "How can we increase our power relative to theirs?" It's not just about getting stronger, it's about making the other side weaker. That's the calculation. That's how they measure success."[1]

In the Party's national security calculus, a win is only a win if China's CNP rises relative to that of its adversaries.

It is an entirely zero-sum worldview.

Where does that zero-sum idea come from? From the original precepts of the communist vision itself. In communist ideology, and within the communist framework laid out by Marx and realized by Lenin, there are only two categories of people: the oppressor and the oppressed. The oppressor *must* struggle against the oppressed.

Nothing exists outside that dynamic.

For many, this may seem counterintuitive; in a capitalist system, a rising tide lifts all boats. Not so in the communist mentality. Indeed, the primary way in which this narrow worldview has traditionally been made so appealing is by insisting on a finite amount of available wealth. The pie is limited, so to speak. And that the only way anyone can become wealthy is by taking a larger piece from someone else. The communist mentality would say that the rich (the oppressor, the owning class) only have everything they have because they've stolen it from *you (the oppressed,* the workers*)*.

There's a kernel of truth there. Yes, some people hoard wealth, and history is full of conquest and exploitation. That much is accurate. But the lie—the dangerous lie, and one we should be teaching children to recognize from a very young age—is that prosperity is somehow fixed. It isn't. What prosperity really means is that you can increase the size of the pie. There are different visions for how to accomplish this, and those visions are often in more or less healthy competition with one another, but the principle is fundamental.

Adam Smith, for example, believed that the division of labor created prosperity: As he wrote in his 1776 work, *An Inquiry into the Nature and Causes of the Wealth of Nations,* "The greatest improvement in the productive powers of labour, and the greater part of the skill, dexterity, and judgment with which it is anywhere directed, or applied, seem to have been the effects of the division of labour."

Why does one person work for another? Because doing so creates value, and often more value than either person could produce alone. Both benefit, and society benefits as well, because something new of worth is created. That's how capitalism is supposed to work. (That model has changed somewhat in the modern, financialized economy, where people make money by manipulating money, often without creating anything of tangible value beyond enriching themselves. Today, the value of the US dollar relies on a government decree rather than being backed by say, gold or another physical commodity. That's a different system altogether. In fact, I'd argue it's closer to socialism than to capitalism.)

The concept that prosperity is potentially infinite is not a particularly difficult one to explain, yet almost no one does. As a biologist, I was never taught where prosperity actually comes from. I went through ten years of university, and not once did anyone try to explain the source of wealth. Given that civilization itself is built on the concept of prosperity, such an educational omission is astonishing.

Without that basic understanding, communist ideologies have been able to mobilize millions on a simple message: These people took from you. They're unfair. Rise up and take back what's yours.

Communism doesn't just advance a zero-sum ideology; it's built on it. By extension, the world itself must be zero-sum.

It's very difficult, in a society where people are taught from birth that communism is real, true, and right, to imagine the world as anything but zero-sum. The pie is limited. If I don't have my share, it's because someone else does.

Some people may study in the West and bring back a broader perspective, and perhaps that helps in certain ways. But ultimately, it's not surprising that they view every relationship with another country through that same zero-sum lens.

So, when the CCP conceives of how it will interact with the rest of the world, it does so entirely through that framework.

EXPORTING ITS SYSTEM

Communism is an inherently internationalist entity; it aims explicitly to export its system. Which is why, when dealing with a communist system, it's essential to understand that its purpose is to spread its ideology until everything is communist. This is a core principle of communism, yet it is not commonly understood in the West.

One could even call it imperialist, though communists would reject that label, claiming instead that they are "fighting" against imperialism. But in practice, the goal is the same. Anything that isn't communist ultimately represents a threat to communism and must be conquered. The Soviet Union worked hard to establish communist regimes (even in countries where it never took hold organically) through pressure, subversion, or outright invasion, for this very reason. The most successful and enduring case is China itself: after the Soviet Union provided massive military, economic, and organizational support to Mao's forces throughout the 1940s, the People's Republic was proclaimed in 1949 and immediately aligned with Moscow until the Sino-Soviet split starting in 1961. Other examples include the direct invasions of Hungary (1956) and Czechoslovakia (1968) to crush reforms that threatened communist control, the arming and training of communist guerrillas across Latin America, Africa, and Southeast Asia, and the decades-long effort to install a puppet regime in Afghanistan, which culminated in the 1979 Soviet invasion.

Free (or at least more free) societies are an existential threat to communism precisely because they hold up a mirror to its failures. They show a better way.

This is why Taiwan poses such a massive problem for Beijing. Taiwan is living proof that the Chinese people can thrive under a free system—its per capita GDP, level of freedom, and quality of life far surpass those of the mainland.

America, then, represents the ultimate adversary—the complete antithesis of communism, of the Party, and of the strategic ambitions laid out in China's "Hundred-Year Marathon." It embodies everything the CCP fears most: individual liberty, faith, and a society grounded in moral principle rather than top-down control. One might argue that the US has strayed considerably from this vision, and one would be correct. Yet it remains *the* place in the world where this vision is still *most* applied today, with tens of millions of people striving to enact it, against all odds.

It's no surprise that Beijing has spent decades working to weaken and undermine the United States—not through open conflict, but through slow, calculated, and often remarkably sophisticated means. This is the essence of the unspoken policy: "hide your strength, bide your time."

The United States—out of naivete, American optimism, ignorance, and yes, greed—has played into China's strategy time and time again.

The roots of this dynamic go back to the Nixon administration and America's rapid opening to China in the 1970s and 1980s. Nixon's play—and Reagan's—was to enlist China as a counterweight to the Soviet Union.

Throughout the first part of the twentieth century, the Soviets had poured resources into China to support both nations' communist expansions, but by that point, they were falling out with each other over rival visions and competing forms of the communist utopia. The United States wisely sought to leverage that split with the idea that China could be made friendly through partnership, business, arms deals, and shared intelligence.

Nixon's calculation, and the logic that guided US–China policy through the Cold War was: use China to balance the Soviet Union. The problem came when the Soviet Union collapsed. Suddenly, there was no longer any strategic need for the relationship.

But by then, the financial and institutional ties between the US and China were deeply entrenched and very difficult to untangle.

Lee Smith, whose book *The China Matrix: The Epic Story of How Donald Trump Shattered a Deadly Pact* explores this in detail and argues that what actually happened was not that America made China more "American," but that we walked straight into a CCP trap: the Party had co-opted America's elites by making them fabulously rich.[2] There's a strong case for that, which we briefly discussed earlier in this book, and Smith lays it out convincingly. When I interviewed Smith about the book, he put it this way: "The way that the China lobby worked was, Kissinger was never paid directly by China. . . . Kissinger was paid by American corporations that wanted to do business in China. So what Kissinger would do was he would take them on long trips to Beijing and they'd be wined and dined. . . . The most influential lobbyists are political donors, people with companies worth billions and billions of dollars. So they're not only making the case for China to the recipients of their donations, they're also telling the people who are getting those donations, you better be nice to China."

By 1989, after the Tiananmen Square massacre, when Chinese troops and tanks crushed pro-democracy demonstrations in Beijing, killing thousands of unarmed students and workers, the relationship had been cemented. Newly declassified material shows that President George H. W. Bush sent Brent Scowcroft to Beijing with a private message: essentially, "We'll help you ride this out."[3] They knew about the massacre, and that event helped Jiang consolidate his rise to power. Jiang had, for years, specialized in co-opting elites—you'll recall that's what the Chinese communists refer to as "wooing the barbarians." He was a master at it.

There's a quintessential moment in Michael Pillsbury's book that captures his own realization of how complicit the United States has become. Pillsbury had worked under Reagan and had delivered weapons to the Chinese as a signal of America's goodwill.[4]

At an event held during the Obama administration—when Hillary Clinton was Secretary of State—a famous Chinese artist known for his elaborate pyrotechnic displays was featured. Michael Pillsbury was there, standing among diplomats and senior officials, as the artist prepared his performance near the White House, not far from the Oval Office.

In a dramatic finale, the artist detonated his creation—a dazzling explosion that obliterated a Christmas tree.

Pillsbury only later understood the symbolism of what he was witnessing.

"Why else would the Smithsonian Institution and the State Department pay a famous Chinese artist $250,000 to blow up a Christmas tree on the National Mall?" he asked during a 2019 interview with Lou Dobbs. "In that moment, I'm not sure that even I appreciated the subversion of the gesture."

To the Chinese hardliners, this was a coup de grâce—a symbolic act of dominance. It was a message: Look how we own the Americans. We're destroying a major American cultural symbol on the lawn of their seat of power. The contempt and symbolism were unmistakable once you understood how the Chinese communists think.

What the CCP had done so effectively was to mislead Americans into believing that China was merely authoritarian, not totalitarian, and, as Kissinger had argued, that it could be slowly transformed into a democracy. That notion wasn't entirely implausible—if you didn't understand how the system actually worked. If you didn't grasp the mechanics of the Chinese Communist system—which, clearly, most didn't—it seemed logical that investment and engagement would lead to liberalization. The prevailing wisdom was that trade would create interdependence, and interdependence would make conflict *less* likely. In short, by doing business together, we'd make war impossible.

That assumption, of course, was catastrophically wrong.

A STRATEGY OF CONCEALMENT

Of course, the Chinese were very good at hiding their true objectives; concealment was part of the strategy. American elites—bankers, business owners, institutional leaders—were lulled (or "wooed," to use the Party's expression) into believing two lies: one was that they, the Americans, were in control, and the other was that China was interested in true partnership. Neither was true, but it worked.

The CCP played to these fictions perfectly. Anytime an American did business in China, for example, they were assigned a handler—a trusted insider who acted as their guide and intermediary. In some cases, the handler was also a honeypot trap. These handlers were experts at creating the impression of partnership: that you're working together toward shared goals, improving the system, and fostering greater cooperation between the two countries.

But in reality, that was almost never true. There may have been a few exceptions—Chinese individuals who genuinely saw themselves as reformers—but overall, there was no real cooperation.

The Party is interested only in control and domination, never in genuine collaboration.

The end result was, essentially, American capture by the Chinese. They owned us.

And as Anders Corr wrote in his book *The Concentration of Power: Institutionalization, Hierarchy & Hegemony*: power ratchets—it only moves in one direction.[5]

Once power consolidates, it tightens; it almost never loosens.

That concept perfectly describes the Chinese Communist Party's approach to partnership with the West. It's the same underlying logic that drives many leftist movements as well: to shift what is abnormal into what is normal, so long as it benefits their side. It's a constant process of small, incremental gains—one ratchet-click at a time—each locking in a new advantage.

Over time, that system, that movement, became the status quo. For two or three decades, that's simply how things worked.

The CCP never really took its eye off the ball.

But for a long time, and maybe still to some extent, America did. We stopped seeing them as adversarial to our own national interests.

In fact, we bent over backwards to avoid doing so. The mantra became: don't do anything that would cause China to lose face—they're too valuable a partner.

Over time, performative language became enough for America. Just saying you were committed to "free trade," "democracy," or "global cooperation" became the functional equivalent of actually doing it—even as the reality moved in the opposite direction.

It's a system that grew almost by inertia. That's how we ended up with, among other things, the artificial reefs being built by CCP dredging machinery, slowly and methodically, over the course of a decade. Beginning around 2013, China dispatched giant cutter-suction dredgers to seven disputed reefs and atolls in the Spratly Islands—Fiery Cross, Subi, Mischief, Cuarteron, Gaven, Hughes, and Johnson South. Over the next five to seven years, these vessels pumped millions of tons of sand and coral onto submerged or barely-exposed features, turning them into full-fledged militarized islands complete with 10,000-foot runways, deep-water ports, radar arrays, missile shelters, and barracks for thousands of troops. Ten years ago, these outposts did not exist in any meaningful military sense; today they are presented by Beijing as if they had always been sovereign Chinese territory. Likewise, when it comes to coal plants, Beijing promises "net zero," yet continues to build coal-fired power stations at a staggering rate—nearly one a day. China now accounts for roughly 85 percent of new global emissions.

James Fanell, a former US Navy commander in the Pacific who was eventually sidelined for being too "China hawkish," co-authored a book with another prominent China analyst, Bradley A. Thayer, senior fellow at the Center for Security Policy, and together they make a compelling case: that there has never been another instance in history where an adversary nation was built into near-dominance by the very country it considers its key enemy.[6]

But that's exactly what happened.

We built it—US money, US ingenuity, US technology, US patents—all of it.

Pillsbury once told me, "Right now, there are twenty departments in the American Embassy in China whose sole job is to transfer technology to China. That's what they do. And that's what they're doing right this second, as we speak. Whatever tech they get, they give it to the Chinese."

And when I asked him, "Why do they keep doing it?" he said simply, "No one's told them to stop."

That's how deep the normalization runs: a system so entrenched, with so many individuals complicit in its crimes on all sides, that even now, it continues by default.

Gordon Chang wrote a deeply insightful book, *The Coming Collapse of China*, in 2001.[7] He boldly predicted that the Chinese Communist Party's authoritarian rule, combined with corruption, inefficient state enterprises, mounting debt, and stifled innovation, would cause economic and political collapse by around 2011. The CCP and the pro-China engagement crowd went to great lengths to discount his analysis when the prediction didn't come true. But his diagnosis of the regime's structural vulnerabilities was fundamentally sound, as we can see in the collapse of China's real estate sector and the many other accumulating visible economic and social problems that the CCP can no longer hide.

Very few of us, really, had the imagination to conceive the sheer scale of Western (mainly US and European) capital inflows to China that were accelerating at exactly this time—which I calculate at roughly 7–12 trillion (yes, with a "t") dollars cumulatively since 1979 through direct investment, supply-chain buildout, technology transfers (forced and voluntary), IP acquisition, education of millions of Chinese scientists and engineers, stock-market and gray-zone market listings, tourism spending, and portfolio flows—that ended up acting as a massive external lifeline, stabilizing the Chinese regime, especially at critical moments. Apple's investments in China alone, as Patrick McGee documents in his *Apple in China*, peaking at $55 billion annually and including a $275 billion five-year pledge, dwarfed those of the entire post-WWII Marshall Plan for Europe (inflation-adjusted). Overall, this enormous transfer of capital and know-how, sustained over decades by the powerful pro-engagement constituency the CCP had cultivated among Western corporate, financial and government elites, bought Beijing far more time than anyone in 2001 could reasonably have foreseen.

Today, the resulting deep economic intertwining has granted the CCP an implicit "too big to fail" status—with trillions in mutual holdings, difficult-to-replace supply chains, and shared financial exposure—giving Beijing tacit blackmail leverage: any sharp collapse, they'll argue, will inflict catastrophic damage on Western economies, pensions, and corporations, making decisive decoupling politically and economically prohibitive. In essence, Gordon Chang correctly identified the deep rot at the core of the Chinese regime, but he didn't realize just how effectively the CCP had figured out how to extract massive value from the West, with the complicity of Western political and corporate leaders, delaying its collapse significantly. He also didn't see that the CCP was masking its true totalitarian nature with an authoritarian façade (as we've discussed), but frankly this is something that remains lost on many China watchers. I myself only fully understood it in recent years.

MAKE THEM COMPLICIT

The Chinese Communist Party has made remarkable progress in exporting its totalitarianism under the guise of "cooperation." Seen through this lens, forced organ harvesting serves several critical purposes for the regime. It guarantees life-extension for Party elites. It fulfills the leadership's directive to eradicate Falun Gong practitioners. And it implicates the West by exploiting our own uneasy history with utilitarian bioethics, from eugenics to other ethically questionable medical experiments. The underlying impulse, in other words, isn't entirely foreign to us.

But part of the CCP's strategy seems unmistakable: to ensure that no one outside China ever tries to dismantle the system. And their method is simple—make everyone complicit. Offer access to what the system provides: organs, data, research partnerships. Once the elites of other nations have benefited, they have no incentive to challenge it. After all, who would sever their own lifeline to a source they may one day depend on? As I wrote in a recent op-ed for the *Baltimore Sun*:

> The US-China transplant connection is extensive. Hundreds of Chinese organ transplant surgeons have trained in major American institutions, from the University of Pittsburgh Medical Center to Mount Sinai Health System, which have formal partnerships with Chinese transplant centers, sharing expertise and giving them a false air of legitimacy. In a May 2025 letter to Harvard's president, the House Select Committee on the CCP wrote that they had "identified multiple instances where Harvard researchers worked with Chinese researchers on organ transplantation-related research"—some of which was NIH-funded. China's transplant industry also relies on Western technology. Most of China's organ preservation solutions, surgical instruments, immunosuppressive drugs

> and transplant diagnostics come from the US or Europe, and fueled China's transplant boom during the height of forced organ harvesting, according to the Institute to Research the Crimes of Communism. All of this casual US engagement with a foreign transplant industry that systemically violates the dead donor rule has led to a softening of ethical protections in the American system. A recent New York Times op-ed by prominent cardiologists that advocates for redefining death to increase organ availability is a case in point.[8]

The genius, and the horror, of the CCP's strategy is that they didn't need to convert us, conquer us, or even challenge us—only to corrupt us. By appealing to our pragmatism, our ambition, our faith in progress and freedom, and yes, our greed, they tempted us to mirror their moral flexibility, and we went along with it. In doing so, we have not only financed their crimes but offered to look the other way.

We have begun to internalize their logic.

CHAPTER 9

UNRESTRICTED WARFARE (AND THE THREE WARFARES)

"WOOING THE BARBARIANS"

The CCP's strategy of *"wooing the barbarians,"* of drawing Western elites into cooperation and complicity, was no accident, nor was it some kind of diplomatic improvisation. It was deliberate, methodical, and central to a broader campaign designed to weaken the West from within: to erode its moral confidence, corrupt its institutions, and make its leaders unwilling or unable to confront the truth of what China has become.

As we've discussed, the Party's success and survival are the paramount purposes of Chinese society. Everything else is subordinate to that objective. Every arm of the system—political, economic, military, academic—is aligned toward a single goal: the preservation and advancement of the Chinese Communist Party. The only relevant question becomes whether an individual, institution, or initiative serves that purpose or undermines it.

Those who act in service of the system may be granted limited autonomy, but it is an autonomy of tactics, not of purpose or strategy.

That distinction—between tactics and purpose—is essential to understanding how the system functions. It shapes every aspect of Chinese life from governance and economics to international relations, and informs how the CCP conceives of warfare, including the ongoing struggle it wages against the West.

This approach was formally articulated in the so-called "Unrestricted Warfare" doctrine, a 1999 military strategy document written by Chinese People's Liberation Army (PLA) Senior Colonels Qiao Liang and Wang Xiangsui. Their thesis was simple but radical: to achieve dominance by employing all means—military and non-military alike—as instruments of warfare. Cyber, economic, legal, and psychological tools could all be weaponized in a limitless, boundary-erasing global conflict.

Qiao and Wang essentially codified a set of lessons and ideas drawn from both traditional Chinese approaches to war, such as those of the Warring States period and the teachings of Sun Tzu, and the evolving strategic thinking of the PLA itself. The result was a kind of manual for waging war without firing a shot. Published openly in 1999, the document has long been available, though largely ignored in the West.

But not by everyone.

General Robert Spalding was among the first American military leaders to take the doctrine seriously. And over the past decade, much of his work has focused on educating the US defense establishment about how the CCP conducts warfare. "The first time I read it in 1999, when it first came out, it was kind of esoteric, a little bit complicated, really sounding crazy, and I really didn't get it in 1999," Spalding told me. "When I came back to the Pentagon, working for the chairman as his advisor on China, I started to get back into documents like 'Unrestricted Warfare,' and I read it again. When you read in the context of 2014, when you have the benefit of almost twenty years of history that has allowed some of the ideas to actually come to fruition, it's a completely different thing."

Spalding gained the insight, shaped by years inside the system, that China is waging war; it simply doesn't resemble what Americans recognize as war.

For the CCP, conflict is constant. It is an unending struggle to expand the reach of communism and suppress all systems that challenge it. Anything that is not communist is, by definition, a threat, and therefore a target for transformation or destruction.

To that end, as Spalding explained, the Party employs every available tool: trade, drugs, lawfare, information and influence operations, cyberattacks, and financial coercion. To Chinese strategists, this is self-evident. To Western military planners, however, Spalding's warnings often seemed baffling. Many dismissed them: "Why are you telling us this? That's an issue for the trade office." Spalding's response was blunt: "Yes, it begins with trade—but it ends with Americans dead, or with the CCP achieving dominance."

It is a completely different way of understanding what "war" means.

The United States is the CCP's primary target, not only because it remains the dominant global power, but because it represents the ideological source of freedom, democracy, and constitutional government. America is the original success story of self-governance against all odds, and therefore the ultimate rival to totalitarian control.

Countries like Canada, which exist within the US security umbrella, are also natural targets. But in the CCP's calculus of "Comprehensive National Power," it is the United States that sets the benchmark—the adversary against which all progress is measured.

The PLA itself is built entirely around this objective. Its structure, strategic priorities, weapons development, and space capabilities are all designed with one overarching goal: to defeat the United States. (And keep in mind that the PLA is not the Chinese army; it is the Party's army, akin to a "Republican Party Army" or a "Democratic Party Army" in the United States.)

In his book, *When China Attacks: A Warning to America*, retired US Marine colonel and China expert Grant Newsham opens the book with a hypothetical scenario of an attack by China on Taiwan.[1] As I read the chapter, I charted numerous unconventional methods of warfare that the CCP utilizes to achieve its objective, including "gray zone" tactics that keep the US confused, unsure if what they're seeing is really a coordinated CCP-led effort, until it's too late. "They do have ways to make life difficult for us . . . like their fishing fleet, the maritime militia, things that look like civilian weapons or civilian entities, and . . . in just about every country, they've got people who put in a good word for them," Newsham told me.[2]

Kinetic warfare is not the CCP's preferred method. It is costly, chaotic, and unpredictable. The CCP's aim is not necessarily to kill, but to control.

People, if they can be controlled, are far more useful alive than dead.

THE THREE WARFARES

Where the CCP has been particularly effective is in the realm of the "Three Warfares": public opinion warfare, psychological warfare, and legal warfare. The Party has invested enormous effort in each, and between Russia and China, they effectively dominate that space, while the United States remains largely absent from it.

Public opinion warfare is about shaping global perception—making the world believe that China is not a threat. One could probably compile an hours-long montage of American commentators and officials repeating the same line: "China's not a threat." That's how effective the messaging has been.

They've spent decades promoting the Kissinger-inspired idea that "you have to get into China." The story goes that an immense consumer market is coming, and if you don't enter now, someone else will. It's worth transferring your intellectual property, because otherwise you'll miss out. And besides, they're "becoming a democracy," so by helping them, you're doing good in the world.

"It started to permeate think tanks, the entire federal government, the State Department, the Defense Department, our literature, and our analysis. The idea was, 'If we engage, things will get better in our relations with China. They will modernize. They will come along and follow the existing international order.' That went on for 40-plus years. During that time, no one ever stopped and asked, 'Is this working?'" James Fanell, retired US Navy captain and former Director of Intelligence and Information Operations for the US Pacific Fleet, told me when I interviewed him and Bradley Thayer about their book, *Embracing Communist China: America's Greatest Strategic Failure*.[3]

Despite all the evidence to the contrary—and there is a lot—many people still believe that today. Perhaps this is the most obvious sign that a successful public opinion warfare campaign has been deployed.

Then there's psychological warfare, of which TikTok is perhaps the most striking and successful example in human history. You couldn't design a more effective psychological weapon than the algorithm behind the so-called social media app.

As I've testified and lectured about extensively, TikTok may be a more powerful weapon than China's nuclear arsenal. It can destabilize and demoralize an entire generation of young people, and arguably already has. It is fully controlled by the CCP and the PLA, yet it is banned in China itself, precisely because they understand what we refuse to acknowledge: how incredibly destructive it is.

They don't want their own youth exposed to it, but are working overtime to expose ours.

It's an extraordinarily effective weapon with built-in plausible deniability. There's periodic talk of transferring TikTok into US ownership, but I don't believe that will ever happen. You don't give away a weapon that powerful.

What the CCP ultimately seeks—and what TikTok can be used to generate and amplify so effectively—is chaos: civil strife, division, and moral disintegration. This is exactly what the former KGB propagandist Yuri Bezmenov, who ultimately defected to the West, described decades ago as the next stage of subversion—the deliberate erosion of a society's ability to think coherently or act collectively.

Look at the recent, tragic Charlie Kirk assassination. Within hours, TikTok was amplifying tailored narratives to polarized audiences. To conservatives, it pushed the idea that Kirk's message had failed and that people should "take matters into their own hands." To left-leaning audiences, it promoted the notion that Kirk was rhetorically so beyond the pale that his death was justified, even worth celebrating. It was the German-American political theorist Herbert Marcuse's concept of "repressive tolerance" in action—the idea that tolerance should only extend to those who advance the "correct" ideology, while others are to be silenced or destroyed.

And then there is legal warfare.

To use the example of TikTok again, the app's parent company, ByteDance, uses elite, "white-shoe" American law firms to manipulate the US legal system. On the surface, it looks no different from Google or Facebook hiring top-tier counsel, navigating regulations, and striking deals. However, the key difference is intent and understanding that intent is the difference between engaging with China and playing the part of the useful idiot for the CCP. For a Chinese firm, there is always a national security objective behind it. These entities are not independent, free-market actors; they are instruments of state power. If such a company is not actively being employed to enact a specific operation, it's always functioning within the confines of CCP objectives, and ready and waiting to spring into action when activated.

Even something as seemingly mundane as legal representation becomes a weapon—an act of legal warfare designed to advance the strategic interests of the CCP. And, again, it is remarkably effective.

At a broader level, the same legal warfare tactic applies to understanding China's entry into the World Trade Organization.

The United States sponsored China's accession in 2001, even though the country had not yet developed the legal or economic frameworks required for membership. It wasn't ready—because it is not, and never will be, a true market economy. Since joining, China has repeatedly violated core WTO rules while maintaining "developing nation" status, and almost no one has successfully held it to account. They have weaponized the very institutions meant to regulate them, turning global trade law into another form of asymmetric (and unrestricted) warfare.

Part of the reason this works so well is that China has managed to co-opt the international system itself. Large global bureaucracies—the UN, WHO, World Bank, and others—often share a technocratic worldview surprisingly compatible with Chinese totalitarianism. Both see society as something to be engineered from above: "We should impose our rules to create a better world." It's not Chinese communism per se, but it reflects the same authoritarian impulse toward control.

As N. S. Lyons argues in his essay "The China Convergence," this shared technocratic mindset has created an odd natural affinity between Western institutions and the CCP.[4] In particular,

Western multilateral and globalist institutions. But beyond shared philosophy, there is also direct influence. In some international agencies, China now holds outright control; in others, it simply exerts enormous pressure.

I heard this directly from a former senior official at the World Bank. When he tried to circulate a memo critical of China, colleagues in the press office stopped him.

"I don't think you can do that," they said.

"Why not?" he asked.

"Because the Chinese won't like it."

Think about it: the World Bank—an ostensibly independent global institution—operating under fear of Beijing's displeasure.

That is legal warfare at scale.

But the CCP's concept of "unrestricted warfare" is not limited to "soft" or covert operations. There is a more aggressive war being waged simultaneously, one that stops shy of all-out traditional war, but has the potential to inflict just as much damage.

That's where the doctrine of military–civil fusion comes in—the idea that anything with potential military application in the civilian sphere must be explored, developed, and integrated into the state's strategic apparatus.

It became an explicit national priority in 2017, likely around the same time the United States began, for the first time, to seriously confront China and recognize the nature of the game being played.

The most immediate and obvious example of that policy in action is the Wuhan Institute of Virology and its gain-of-function research, which became infamous as a potential source of the COVID-19 virus.

For anyone remotely familiar with the field, gain-of-function research, defined as making viruses more virulent or more transmissible, has clear military implications. Everyone in that space understands it, even if they don't say so publicly, because it's inconvenient for funding and approval. The goal, after all, is to make a pathogen *more* functional. That's what "gain of function" means.

So, of course, such work has military application. It is, in effect, the weaponization of biology.

That's why the question "Was the Wuhan Institute of Virology military-linked?" is almost absurd on its face. Even in the United States, there's no version of this kind of research that proceeds without at least some military interest or oversight. Any experiment that makes a virus more lethal or transmissible automatically falls under the purview of national defense.

Once you understand the military–civil fusion doctrine, the answer is obvious: yes, it's a military lab. There's no other scenario. You don't need special proof. If the work can be weaponized, it falls under the military system by definition.

China's regime maintains an active, high-priority bioweapons program, and this type of research fits squarely within it.

You can see the same logic in action with drone technology. Suppose a drone company partners with an American firm. On paper, it's a commercial enterprise—for photography, agriculture, or mapping. But in China, every such technology is dual-use by default. Military applications must be explored. That's one of Xi Jinping's top national priorities.

Failing to pursue that angle would mark a person—or a company—as politically unreliable, someone not fully aligned with the system. That's unthinkable. Everyone is expected to serve the same overarching strategic purpose.

The West's general misunderstanding of this policy has been deeply problematic. American firms still believe they can safely partner with "private" Chinese companies, provided they see no explicit military ties. Legal departments go to great lengths to prove that such companies are not part of the PLA or under CCP control. But under military–civil fusion, that distinction simply doesn't exist.

Every Chinese company is part of the system. And it's reasonable to assume that any partnership with a Chinese entity has military implications—100 percent of the time.

Why? Because every partnership is an opportunity: to steal technology, co-opt personnel, and subvert the Party's chief adversary.

And in the grim calculus of a potential Taiwan invasion, recall how this fusion can enable atrocities: earlier in this book I related how former Chinese military doctor Dr. Zheng Zhi leaked details from the PLA's annually updated combat plans, with surrendered Taiwanese soldiers to be used as "living sources" for blood, skin grafts, and organs to sustain wounded Chinese troops, with mobile, containerized "field hospital" units deployed for on-site extraction. This plan builds on the vision and logistics of the CCP's forced organ harvesting industry, reducing a new cohort of lives to utilitarian statistics for the "greatest good" as defined by the Party elite. Under Military-Civil Fusion, the elements of China's forced organ harvesting system will support these battlefield logistics.

CHAPTER 10

THE MAGIC WEAPON

THE UNITED FRONT WORK DEPARTMENT

Considering its doctrine of "unrestricted warfare" and its goal of domination, it's no surprise that the CCP operates a vast and intricate network of influence operations designed to shape global public opinion about China, the Party, and international responses to its actions.

Central to this effort is the United Front Work Department (UFWD), one of the Party's most powerful and least understood institutions. Mao Zedong identified the UFWD as one of the "three magic weapons" of the communist revolution, alongside armed struggle and party-building. And decades after Mao's death, the UFWD remains a cornerstone of the regime's strategy for maintaining control at home and expanding influence abroad.

It is crucial to understand how this institution operates.

The primary goal of the UFWD, domestically and internationally, is to co-opt elites, dissidents, ethnic and religious minorities, and the Chinese diaspora, to neutralize opposition, gather intelligence, and extend the Party's reach into every sphere of global life.

It is essential to the CCP's stability and dominance, and it operates on a scale that has virtually no parallel in the West.

Much of its focus begins with Chinese communities overseas. Here, the Party's racial and ideological worldview comes into play. The CCP sees itself not only as a communist supremacist movement but also as a Han supremacist one. Han is the largest ethnic group in China, and indeed the world. The CCP regards Han Chinese, whether living in China or abroad, as belonging to the Chinese state. Non-Han peoples within China are often treated with contempt and occupy lower social status, yet abroad, all ethnic Chinese are viewed as part of Beijing's extended political family—subjects, in effect, of Party authority.

The UFWD is extraordinarily well-funded and expansive. Its operations hide in plain sight. In countries across the West, including the United States, authorities have identified what are colloquially called "Chinese police stations." These are often small offices or storefronts, sometimes operating out of legitimate businesses in Chinatown districts. In reality, they are extensions of the UFWD.

Personnel working in or with these offices act as community enforcers, tasked with monitoring and intimidating diaspora members. A Falun Gong practitioner running a "Quit the CCP" stand in Flushing, New York, might suddenly face harassment or organized disruption. Activists are often confronted by individuals claiming to "represent the embassy," warning them that their actions "hurt the feelings of the Chinese people." These seemingly local actors function as informal agents of Beijing, ensuring that Chinese communities abroad remain compliant and self-policing. (For the best overview of CCP's strategy behind its influence operations in the US, see John Lenczowski's seminal piece, "Conquest Without War: The Threat of Chinese Political Influence Operations," in *The Intelligencer Journal of US Intelligence Studies*.)[1]

TRANSNATIONAL REPRESSION

In 2022, most likely in part in anticipation of Cheng Pei Ming—the lone forced organ harvesting survivor—going public with his story, and desperately wanting to undermine it, Xi Jinping issued a special directive at the level of the Minister of State Security. The directive's purpose was explicit: to eliminate Falun Gong operations overseas.[2] By which he meant, aside from Falun Gong practitioners' individual activities, the operations of large media companies founded by Falun Gong practitioners—*The Epoch Times* and NTD Television—and the traditional Chinese dance company Shen Yun, all major thorns in the CCP's side.

The United Nations refers to such acts as "transnational repression"—the regime's efforts to exert pressure, intimidation, and surveillance beyond its own territory—targeting dissidents, exiles, journalists, and activists overseas in order to control narratives and suppress dissent.

At the time, we at *Epoch* didn't know the directive existed; we only noticed a sudden increase in harassment, interference, and strange activity directed toward us.

Later, we learned the truth—from Yuan Hongbing, a Chinese dissident and former law professor at Peking University, who supported student activists after the 1989 Tiananmen Square massacre, for which he was jailed and later exiled to Australia. He maintains a network of students still inside China, quietly feeding him information under the cover of darkness.

According to his sources, the regime had anticipated a wave of mainstream attention and instructed its operatives to use American institutions, wherever possible and under the cloak of plausible deniability, to discredit and destroy the messenger.

Of course, it wasn't my first experience with the Party's intimidation machine.

For anyone working to expose the Party's crimes, cyberattacks are so frequent that you become desensitized to them. It's simply part of the operating environment. And it's not just cyberattacks: there are hacking attempts, DDoS assaults, phishing campaigns, and harassment of reporters' families in China—layers of pressure designed to disrupt, intimidate, and exhaust. Transnational repression in action.

What's so audacious is how normal it's become. Just as siphoning American intellectual property became normal, or manipulating Western institutions became normal, targeting independent media abroad has become, for the CCP, standard operating procedure.

The repressions manifest in many ways. During the Hong Kong protests in 2019, for example, *The Epoch Times* printing presses were firebombed, an unmistakable act of intimidation meant to silence us.[3] (It's worth remembering that the CCP effectively took Hong Kong during the COVID pandemic—yet another example of how the Party weaponized the pandemic. The lockdowns and chaos conveniently neutralized the pro-democracy movement. It was a perfect storm: the state response to the virus halted mass protests, and the CCP moved quickly to consolidate control. The CCP would never use the word annexation to describe what it did in Hong Kong—because in their view, it already belonged to them—but that's precisely what happened. The "one country, two systems" promise, which had been eroding for years, was effectively scrapped overnight. The Party declared full authority, and anyone who had been politically active or outspoken was arrested.)

But it was not just *The Epoch Times* as a media outlet that was targeted on Xi's orders. It was Falun Gong in general. From their point of view, it's simple: if the CCP has the United Front Work Department to run influence operations, then *The Epoch Times*, which was founded by Falun Gong practitioners, must be the Falun Gong equivalent. That's how they think—everything must be at its center an influence structure, because that's how their own system works.

From the CCP's perspective, *The Epoch Times* is remarkably effective at exposing CCP bad behavior (this is one of the few points on which CCP operatives and I strongly agree, in fact!), much as Falun Gong practitioners are, and it needed to be silenced.

The Epoch Times was founded by a group of Chinese Americans, many of whom had come through the 1989 student movement in China and later found their way to Georgia Tech University on scholarships. They settled in Atlanta and, like many others who left around that time, never went back. They weren't the top leaders of the movement, but they had seen enough to understand what the regime was, and they decided to stay under the radar in the United States.

In 1999, when the persecution of Falun Gong began and Jiang Zemin's state-driven propaganda machine turned against practitioners, they recognized what was happening. From America—protected by the First Amendment—they felt a responsibility to speak out. The world was hearing only the CCP's version of events—that Falun Gong was evil, that members were predatory, that it was a "heretical religion" that the CCP quickly translated in English as the highly pejorative "cult" moniker—and much of the Western press was unknowingly repeating Party talking points as if they were legitimate "perspectives."

So in 2000, they launched *The Epoch Times* as a response—to tell the other side of the story, to document what was truly happening in China. In their eyes, the next major chapter of Communist Party persecution was underway: first it was the students in 1989, then Falun Gong a decade later.

The idea resonated with readers. When there's a void of real information and suddenly a source appears that's willing to tell the truth, people flock to it. The paper grew quickly, becoming widely read in Chinese communities around the world.

Before long, they realized they also needed to reach an English-speaking audience, and by 2003, *The Epoch Times* expanded into

English. In the first few years, the focus was on China—covering human rights abuses, the corruption in the Party, and the CCP threat to America—but as readership grew, it quickly evolved into a much broader publication. Perhaps influenced by the health benefits associated with Falun Gong, one of the most popular sections in *The Epoch Times* in its early years (wildly popular to this day!) was its evidence-based alternative health section, featuring integrative medicine, naturopathy, Traditional Chinese Medicine (TCM) i.e. acupuncture, as well as more conventional approaches to staying healthy.

Around the same time, another media company, New Tang Dynasty (NTD) Television, was founded in New York. It began independently, with a similar mission, but focused on television instead of print. Within just a few years, NTD had secured satellite time and was broadcasting directly into mainland China—the old-fashioned way, before streaming became dominant. (Online media was still small then, but over time, that dynamic flipped.)

In 2016, *The Epoch Times* and NTD formally became sister organizations. They didn't merge, but began sharing resources—production teams, staff, facilities, and strategy—forming a kind of multimedia ecosystem. That context is key to understanding how transnational repression operates against us as a media network.

On the television side, in particular, the CCP found ways to leverage Western corporations to interfere, whether volitionally or not. At one point, the CCP struck a deal with International Media Distribution (IMD), a wholly owned subsidiary of Comcast that handled the distribution of international channels on US cable networks, to carry its state propaganda outlets like CGTN. As designed by the regime, this arrangement granted the CCP indirect access to and de facto support from America's largest cable operator. For years, it seemed impossible to negotiate direct carriage deals for NTD, effectively suppressing the independent,

CCP-critical broadcaster while amplifying Beijing's narratives to millions of households.

Before the consolidation of cable (and fiber) TV companies, there were many independent cable systems. Getting carriage on those networks was vital for NTD—channels earned revenue based on the number of potential viewers, not actual ones. Consultants specialized in securing distribution deals. Sometimes the cable provider paid the channel; other times, smaller networks paid for placement to gain exposure.

That was the environment NTD operated in, and it's where the CCP found its pressure point. Before long, Chinese state television CCTV had fully penetrated the American cable system—in Chinese, English, even Spanish. Once CCTV secured those slots, they would issue an unspoken demand: if CCTV was on, NTD could not be.

There were a few exceptions—local systems where NTD managed to get limited carriage—but overall, it was extraordinarily difficult. We learned that executives inside those systems had been conditioned to believe NTD was "anti-China," "illegitimate," or even "evil." That narrative had been seeded at the top, often by industry peers under CCP influence or pay. I spoke years ago with top cable industry executives, and in two specific cases discovered that the CCP had been effective at seeding anti-Falun Gong propaganda at the highest echelons of the industry, i.e. they had come to believe the CCP narratives. But things appear to be changing, as NTD is now being carried on Comcast in several cable markets.

It sounds far-fetched, but it's easy to imagine how this would have played out in real life. You, an NTD representative, go into an advertising meeting and say, "We reach 60 percent of the Chinese market in America." The buyer is thrilled—that's a huge audience. Until you add: "Before we sign, you'll probably get a call from someone claiming to represent the Chinese government.

They'll tell you we're evil, and that you shouldn't work with us. But we're not—we stand for freedom, democracy, rule of law, and faith."

You can guess how many deals survived that conversation. Maybe one in a hundred. Most advertisers aren't willing to risk the wrath of the Chinese regime.

That's just one example of the persecution *The Epoch Times* and NTD face. But it illustrates the CCP's strategy: not just slander and intimidation, but a systemic, layered campaign to suppress, isolate, and economically cripple independent Chinese media abroad.

Looking at Shen Yun, the classical Chinese dance company, you find another version of the same story.

In a sense, Shen Yun is an American dream story—just like *The Epoch Times*. Despite the regime's relentless attempts to crush it through blacklisting, intimidation, and influence campaigns, it has become wildly successful. Even with one of the world's most powerful authoritarian regimes trying to stop it, they still built it, because this is America, and here you can create something from nothing.

The idea behind Shen Yun was to revive traditional Chinese dance, and through it, revive traditional Chinese culture and storytelling, especially the ancient legends and moral tales nearly erased during the Cultural Revolution. The founders of Shen Yun, also Falun Gong practitioners, sought out teachers who still remembered fragments of those traditions; they came from mainland China, Taiwan, and even from Russian gymnastics, which had absorbed some of those movements during the period of CCP–Soviet cooperation.

They brought it all together into an extraordinary performance: Chinese classical and ethnic dance, accompanied by a live orchestra blending Western and Chinese instruments, creating something both authentic and accessible to modern audiences—with a tinge of exposing the CCP's crimes, and as I read it, with a subtext of, "all of the great things about China in fact have nothing to do with the CCP."

Today, Shen Yun reaches over a million people every year, with eight touring companies traveling the world. They've even built a complete academy system—elementary, high school, and university—all from nothing. It's remarkable by any standard.

The CCP has tried to stop Shen Yun, whose tagline is "China Before Communism," for years—calling theaters, pressuring venues, slashing bus tires, and harassing staff and dancers. The regime's obsession with suppressing Shen Yun is deep and enduring, driven by both ideological hostility and fear of what it represents: a living, breathing reminder of China's true cultural heritage—the one the CCP tried to destroy.

Their interference almost always operates just below the threshold of open violence—a "tolerable level" of repression, always with plausible deniability. But the list of incidents is long: cyberattacks, coordinated threats, intimidation, and in some cases, actual violence. It's a litany of the ways the CCP reaches across borders to silence voices it cannot control.

THE CCP PLAYBOOK: SLANDER AND DISCREDIT

Xi was not wrong to anticipate an enormous amount of attention on Cheng Pei Ming—a survivor of forced organ harvesting, is going to be a big story no matter how hard the Party worked to discredit it.

When Cheng finally did go public with his story, the regime's machinery really kicked into gear. Their reaction was entirely predictable and emblematic of how the CCP responds to any accusation, whether it concerns the Uyghurs in concentration camps, expert reports on mass detentions, or even the US government's genocide declaration.

The script is always the same: "These are lies and rumors spread by Western anti-China forces." That's the first response—deny everything and blame foreign hostility. Then come the media smear campaigns. What's especially notable about the organ-harvesting issue, however, is that the regime almost never talks about it at all. Their standard approach has been silence.

The one early exception came after the first major allegations—when journalists reported on the Sujiatun concentration camp. Recall that the regime staged a Potemkin-style inspection, inviting foreign observers to tour a fake facility and declare everything normal. Since then, CCP officials have stayed almost entirely quiet, save for the occasional comment from Huang Jiefu, the former vice minister of health and CCP lead on transplantation PR: "Yes, we used prisoners, it was terrible, but we stopped."

That's the official line—acknowledge just enough to appear transparent, then declare the issue closed. They never engage the substance of the evidence; they simply repeat that it's all "anti-China lies."

But this time was different. The emergence of a living survivor was so threatening that the CCP launched a state-level attack campaign eerily similar to the propaganda blitz they waged against Falun Gong in the early 2000s.

The playbook was identical: slander and discredit. The victim is insane. The victim is evil. The victim is a CIA asset. The story is Falun Gong propaganda. It's all lies. On and on. It's essentially a form of cancellation—both inside China and internationally—a systematic attempt to erase a person's credibility and existence.

But in Cheng's case, that was much harder to do. There was physical, medical evidence—scans showing his liver had partially regenerated, and part of his lung was gone. The facts could not be dismissed.

The regime then concocted a bizarre counter-narrative. They claimed that because Cheng had swallowed a nail and a razor blade, doctors had performed emergency surgery with his consent to save him from self-harm. However, the story didn't add up; the surgery clearly made no sense as surgical action that might have been taken to protect Cheng.

"As the record shows, they didn't need to go into his side all the way around his back and through his chest. They could have gone down into his esophagus with an endoscope and pulled everything out. They were fishing," former US Assistant Secretary of State for Democracy, Human Rights, and Labor Robert Destro, who rescued Cheng to America, told me. Cheng's family also flatly denied their consent: "That's insane; we would never have allowed that," they had stated. None of this made any sense.[4]

Ironically, in trying to cover up the crime, the regime confirmed key details—that Cheng had been detained, hospitalized, and surgically operated on. "They confirmed that the surgery happened. They confirmed where it happened. They confirmed when it happened," said Destro. That acknowledgment alone is unprecedented.

"We were able to get Mr. Cheng into the United States, and we were able to get independent experts to look inside and see what's missing. We confirmed that part," said Destro.

CHAPTER 11

TRANSNATIONAL COOPERATION, CORRUPTION, AND COERCION

CHINA AND THE WORLD HEALTH ORGANIZATION

The United Front Work Department (UFWD) played a critical role in the CCP's original rise to power—its job was to persuade and manipulate people into compliance and loyalty. That mission continues today. It now targets overseas community leaders, academics, businesspeople, journalists, and policymakers—anyone capable of influencing how China is perceived or how governments respond to its behavior.

Other branches of the regime—the People's Liberation Army (PLA) and the Ministry of State Security (MSS)—have their own intelligence and influence units. But the UFWD's sole focus is ideological and psychological warfare: influence and co-option on a global scale. Within the CCP, it is still referred to as a "magic weapon"—a tool of extraordinary power that allows the Party to shape opinion, gather intelligence, and project control far beyond its borders.

The reach of the UFWD doesn't end with diaspora communities or sympathetic elites. Its influence extends deep into the world's most powerful international institutions—organizations that shape global policy, public health, and even moral authority.

Over time, the CCP has learned that it doesn't need to dominate these bodies by force; it only needs to embed itself within them, aligning their missions with the Party's worldview. The goal isn't necessarily to control every decision, but to ensure that when critical moments arise, these institutions speak and act in ways that serve Beijing's interests.

Few examples illustrate this more clearly than the World Health Organization, whose leadership and response to China during the COVID-19 pandemic revealed just how deeply that influence runs.

The man who runs the World Health Organization, Tedros Adhanom Ghebreyesus, is, first of all, a communist, or at least he openly describes himself as a socialist. And second, he was China's choice for that position. You can see how that's played out. Many within the organization are aligned with Beijing's interests as well, and that didn't happen overnight.

It was part of a deliberate, long-term strategy to co-opt international institutions and bend them toward the Party's goals. The CCP accomplished this, in part, by appealing to shared instincts: "We're on your side. We're social engineers too. And we're the only ones who can really make this work. Those Americans, with their First Amendment and liberty talk, they get in the way. They stop the plan." This strategy has led to the WHO doing things that seem completely irrational—like praising the CCP's "zero-COVID" approach or ignoring early warnings from Taiwan that the virus was contagious while the CCP still denied it and allowed international travel. The organization simply accepted Beijing's line—that the virus wasn't contagious between humans, without question. "While the WHO is supposed to support the entire world, during the COVID-19 pandemic, it appeared to protect its relationship with the CCP. The WHO was misinformed, denied access to China, and was used as cover for the CCP's reckless actions," reads the "After Action Review of the COVID-19 PANDEMIC: The Lessons Learned and a Path Forward" report by the House Special Subcommittee on the Coronavirus Pandemic.[1]

These weren't small mistakes. They had profound global consequences, and they stem directly from how effective the UFWD and related influence networks have been at co-opting key international bodies, most notably the WHO.

Public health, in particular, has emerged as a powerful arena for CCP influence. The reasons for this are obvious: once a public health emergency is declared, authorities can assume quasi-dictatorial powers, no matter how "free" the society. In China, of course, that's second nature—they exercised those powers during COVID in ways that shocked even many Chinese citizens. But even in the West, we learned how easily the language of "public health" can be used to justify extraordinary, top-down control.

That realization that public health can become a tool of governance made it a perfect target for CCP infiltration and influence. They recognized that early and exploited it. One can see it in the kinds of policies and people being promoted: pro-CCP, pro–top-down, pro–extreme control. Ideas that once seemed fringe are now accepted as standard pandemic management.

For years, the West had thoughtful, balanced public health policies grounded in proportionality and civil liberty. But when the time came, those principles were swiftly abandoned—replaced by something far closer to the CCP model.

Some of the most effective UFWD operations have been

carried out by Dr. Huang Jiefu, the public face of China's organ transplant industry.

Even in communist societies, leadership has to create a moral pretext for hurting people. There has to be a good reason to do bad things. When it came to the Party's campaign to eradicate Falun Gong, people were made to believe they were evil and dangerous, and every sector of society was expected to contribute to the goal of eliminating them. It was for the greater good of the nation.

Within the medical establishment, the question became: how does our profession serve the eradication directive? For psychiatry, the answer was to use its tools to "cure" people of their beliefs—to break them, to treat them out of being Falun Gong.

That translated into psychiatric torture in various forms. Practitioners were injected with unknown drugs. Many lost control of their bodies, suffered violent seizures, or endured terrifying physical reactions. Electroconvulsive therapy (ECT) was also used, but unlike legitimate medical use, it was administered without anesthesia. It was torture, plain and simple. Per an *Epoch Times* report citing a 2007 incident:

"You will no longer shout after I give you a shot," said the director of the Hebei Provincial Brainwashing Center in China, while threatening Falun Gong practitioner Hua Fengxiang, who kept saying out loud, "Falun Gong is good!" Yuan Shuqian, who has been serving as the director of the brainwashing center since 2001, ordered his officers to stuff a towel in Hua's mouth before forcibly injecting him with an unidentified drug. Shortly after the shot, Hua's health deteriorated, his spine became distorted, his neck became stiff, and he had difficulty walking, reported Minghui.org.[2]

The difference, at least early on, was that this abuse wasn't hidden as carefully, and unlike with forced organ harvesting, many victims survived. Enough that eventually, the international psychiatric community intervened. The World Psychiatric Association

(WPA), pressured the Chinese Society of Psychiatrists (CSP) over documented psychiatric abuses against Falun Gong practitioners. They reportedly said: "This is horrific. If you continue, we'll cut you off—you'll lose your memberships, your international standing, your partnerships—everything."

Under that pressure, the Chinese authorities appeared to reduce the use of this means of persecution. The general belief was that the psychiatric abuse campaign had been halted, at least publicly, as a result of international outrage. For a time, it seemed like a rare win—a case where global pressure actually forced the regime to back down.

But recent reports suggest that may not be true—that the practice simply went underground. A November 2025 United Kingdom Government Country Policy and Information Note (CPIN) on Falun Gong states that detained practitioners face "forced drug administration" in psychiatric hospitals to undermine their faith, classified as torture. It asserts with evidence that abuses have "continued systematically" since 1999, with limited evidence of stopping after the early interventions.[3]

THE PONTIFICAL ACADEMY OF SCIENCES SUMMIT ON ORGAN TRAFFICKING AND TRANSPLANT TOURISM

In stark contrast, the CCP's transplant abuses were effectively endorsed by the international community. The Transplantation Society (TTS), instead of condemning China's actions, essentially gave them the green light.

The international community's complicity was on full display in February 2017, when the Vatican's Pontifical Academy of Sciences convened a two-day summit on organ trafficking. Gathering more than eighty leading transplant surgeons, health officials, and legal experts from across the world, the summit was part of Pope Francis's commendable effort to confront modern forms of human exploitation and recognize organ trafficking as a crime against humanity.

Tellingly, however, China's delegation was led by Dr. Huang Jiefu, former vice minister of health and chair of China's national organ transplant committee. In his remarks, Dr. Huang categorically denied that the country continued to source organs from prisoners or ethnic minorities, asserting that since January 1, 2015, "voluntary civilian organ donors" had been the nation's sole legitimate source. His participation, which had to have been authorized at the highest levels of the Party, was perhaps meant to signal that China had reformed its transplant system.

In reality, it had the opposite effect.

Dr. Jacob Lavee, who you'll recall was among the first to expose the CCP's forced organ harvesting, publicly challenged Huang's claims, noting that no Chinese law had ever explicitly prohibited the use of prisoner organs.[4] DAFOH issued a statement condemning the Vatican's inclusion of the Chinese delegation, calling Beijing's assurances a "mask of deception" unsupported by any independent verification.[5]

Far from quieting concerns, the 2017 Vatican summit spotlighted a profound gap: between China's self-proclaimed reform and the Party's half-hearted lip service to human rights, and the international demand for transparency. It revealed how Beijing's campaign to legitimize its transplant system depends not only on domestic propaganda, but also on the complicity, or at best, the wishful thinking, of institutions abroad.

The relationships between senior Chinese health officials and leaders of international transplant organizations were cultivated over many years. These relationships have often been exploited not by the global medical community to hold Beijing accountable, but by the Chinese Communist Party to legitimize and obscure its system of forced organ harvesting.

Beginning in 2005, Dr. Francis Delmonico, a leading figure in international transplant medicine and former president of TTS, entered into a long-standing partnership with Dr. Huang. The collaboration, framed as a reform effort, spanned more than a decade and included multiple visits by Delmonico to Chinese transplant centers—visits that Beijing would later cite as evidence of international endorsement for its claims of ethical progress.

When Dr. Huang announced in December 2014 that China would stop sourcing organs from prisoners as of January 1, 2015, Delmonico took the news largely at face value, calling it a "seminal event" in global transplant reform—even though there was no independent verification, no new law, and no real oversight to prove anything had changed.

A few years later, Delmonico helped organize the 2017 Vatican summit and personally pushed Vatican officials to invite representatives from Beijing, insisting that China was "part of the solution."[6] Even after the backlash, Delmonico stood by the decision, saying he would "lead the conference the same way" and "wouldn't have the meeting without them." In practice, the Party has been able to use Delmonico's collaboration to strengthen, not reform, the system. He helped design a new national organ classification that in effect blurred the line between brain death and cardiac death, supposedly to "overcome cultural barriers" to donation. Critics said it simply gave cover to the same unethical practices under a new name. He also helped roll out donation after brain death and circulatory death (DBCD), a procedure that made transplants more efficient by extending the window for organ retrieval—but again, without addressing the moral problem at the core of it all.

Even so, Delmonico continued to state that China had made progress toward reform, while admitting he couldn't "assure" anyone that the use of prisoner organs had really stopped. His focus stayed on executed prisoners, leaving the much darker issue—the systematic harvesting of organs from prisoners of conscience, like Falun Gong practitioners, Uyghurs, and other persecuted groups—largely untouched.

Institutionally, TTS introduced a narrow "academic boycott," refusing to publish Chinese studies that used prisoner data. But many saw this as window dressing, knowing China could easily tweak its reporting and continue on as before. By continuing to give Chinese officials platforms at major conferences and treating them as credible reformers, TTS and its leaders helped reinforce Beijing's narrative of progress, lending a sense of legitimacy to a system that, in reality, had never changed.

That's because the Party has no intention of changing the system, and they never have. Instead, it is content to keep turning goodwill into complicity. From United Front Work Department operations, to high-profile "summits" like the Vatican conference, to the long pattern of Western collaboration with China's transplant system, the Party has waged a quiet war on our moral legitimacy.

A scenario I recently learned about from surgeon Dr. Andreas Weber, a former team member of a surgical organ harvesting team and now head of DAFOH Germany, illustrates this at the personal level:

An affluent German woman from Mönchengladbach, with the rare AB blood type, struggled with alcoholism for years, and faced liver failure. In systems like Germany's, finding a match might take years, or not happen at all. Yet she obtained three livers in China around 2015–2019, each in just months, for approximately $400,000, involving a visit to China for each procedure. Her continued drinking, combined with anti-rejection medications, led to quick rejections of each liver—one about every two years.

This was likely facilitated, says Weber, by informal links with the University of Essen, a major transplant center in the Eurotransplant zone, which had listed partnerships with China on living liver donor research—but were removed from their site after his letter explained the connection of the Chinese transplant system to persecutions of Falun Gong, Uyghurs, and Christians. A few months later, he learned that cooperation had quietly resumed in 2025, with Chinese doctors present for immunology and anti-rejection work.

The CCP's ultimate goal? To normalize the abnormal; to make crimes look like progress; to offer the unthinkable in service of our vices, and to ensure that anyone capable of exposing the truth becomes, in some way, compromised.

The result is not just a distortion of reality and the preservation of a system built on human rights abuses, but a steady erosion of moral authority—all in service of a single aim: the global advance of communism and the survival of the Party itself.

CHAPTER 12

FATAL ATTRACTION: HOW THE US PERCEIVES THE CCP

WHERE DID WE GO WRONG AND WHY DOES IT MATTER?

The fatal flaw of the United States has been not seeing the Chinese Communist Party as it truly is, but as we imagine it could be.

As discussed earlier, the Kissinger Doctrine, which called for integrating China into the global system as a counterweight to the Soviet Union, was a mistake on every level. The theory that by increasing diplomatic and economic engagement with China, the country would gradually become more open, more free, and ultimately, more American was based on profound misunderstandings of Chinese goals, history, and the nature of communist ideology itself.

What the Kissinger Doctrine *actually* did was create a framework through which the United States financed and facilitated China's rise. While America transferred its industrial base and critical supply chains to China, the CCP cheated, deceived, and manipulated every good-faith offering to serve its own ambitions.

In effect, even after the United States built China into what it is today, the long-promised democratization never came.

Instead, Washington made a series of disastrous concessions—turning a blind eye to human rights abuses, overlooking forced labor, mass surveillance, and political repression—all while convincing itself that change was just over the horizon. One could argue, though not convincingly in my opinion, that from the American perspective, we're still waiting for the results Kissinger promised: liberalization, genuine partnership, a freer, more "Western" China.

But from the CCP's perspective—from the vantage point of its "Hundred-Year Marathon"—the United States has naively played into its hands every step of the way.

So where did we go wrong? And, more importantly, why does it still matter?

There are different answers to those questions.

One comes from the theory Lee Smith put forward in his essay "The Thirty Tyrants," which formed the basis of his later book *The China Matrix*.[1] He compares the relationship between China and the United States to that of Sparta and Athens in the ancient world. When Sparta conquered Athens, it didn't govern directly; it installed thirty Athenian leaders—the Thirty Tyrants—who ruled in name but were ultimately owned by Sparta. Smith argues that today's American elites have assumed a similar role: outwardly powerful, but effectively captured by China's influence.

Smith elaborates that this capture began accelerating after China's 2001 entry into the World Trade Organization, which flooded the US with cheap goods and created a lucrative market for American companies, fostering a dependency that turned elites into proxies for Beijing's interests. Smith continues to detail how this manifests across sectors: Wall Street firms like Blackstone profited immensely from Chinese investments while lobbying against tariffs; Hollywood self-censored films to appease Beijing's censors; and elite universities, such as Harvard, accepted billions in Chinese donations that influenced curricula and silenced criticism of the CCP. Ultimately, Smith contends this elite comprador class has betrayed American sovereignty, prioritizing personal enrichment over national security, as he observes: "The American elite class has effectively been conquered by the Chinese Communist Party—not through invasion, but through the irresistible lure of money and the abdication of responsibility."

I place more of the onus on the CCP itself, but I think it's really both—a moral cancer of sorts that spreads in all directions. The CCP's major breakthrough, in my view, was realizing just how easily the West could be controlled and manipulated when money was involved. As Mark Twain famously observed, "It's difficult to get a man to understand something when his salary depends upon his not understanding it." When financial incentives enter the picture, even the most principled societies lose clarity. This is especially true in America, a capitalist powerhouse where the pursuit of wealth is not just encouraged but celebrated as a core virtue—anyone can rise from rags to riches through ingenuity and hard work, fostering innovation, economic growth, and individual freedom. Yet, this same strength has a dark underbelly: unchecked greed became an Achilles' heel, easily exploited by the CCP, which spent decades dangling lucrative deals to bend decisions, eroding ethical boundaries, and encouraging extreme prioritizing short-term profits over long-term growth and national security.

You can picture it: American bankers and executives flying to Beijing, hearing exactly what they want to hear. Millions of dollars. Zero risk. Free money.

Henry Kissinger's policy had already given the whole project a veneer of legitimacy—a moral gloss that made engagement with a totalitarian regime seem not only permissible but strategic.

From there, another idea took hold—one even more seductive: You have to get into China. Outsource everything. Manufacture everything there. If you had the right connections and greased the right palms, you could secure your access and tell yourself it was simply good business. But it wasn't just good business. It wasn't just cheaper. And it wasn't just that the regulatory environment was less restrictive than anywhere else. You—the American businessman—were working for the greater good. Americanization, the spread of democracy. We can show them how effective capitalism can be.

A mania developed—an economic fever that swept through boardrooms, think tanks, and governments alike—and it blinded a lot of people.

But not everyone. Some saw the writing on the wall.

Congressman Chris Smith, in particular, emerged as one of the early voices of resistance. After the Tiananmen Square massacre, he fought hard against granting China Most Favored Nation (MFN) trade status. He understood that engaging economically with a regime that gunned down its own students in the streets would have consequences, not just moral, but geopolitical.[2]

At the time, there was still a human rights contingency attached to the trade agreement: China had to demonstrate progress on basic human rights before enjoying preferential access to US markets. But that linkage didn't last.

President Bill Clinton eventually decoupled human rights from trade, striking a deal with the CCP that removed the moral conditions altogether, and MFN status was granted nonetheless. It was one of the most disastrous policy decisions of the modern era. As Congressman Chris Smith recounted to me in 2022, he had been deeply involved in efforts to tie China trade to human rights improvements: "Bill Clinton on May 26th, 1994, de-linked human rights from trade. That's when the Chinese Communist Party said, 'These guys are bluffers. They are fake.' I put that right at the Chinese Communist Party," he said. Smith described how, prior to this, there had been annual battles in Congress over MFN renewal, with human rights conditions attached, but Clinton's decision marked a turning point: "For decades, both Democrats and Republicans had argued that by opening trade with China, China would gradually become more like the West and adopt liberal, democratic values." Instead, this decoupling empowered the regime, allowing atrocities to escalate without economic repercussions, as the CCP correctly perceived US commitments as hollow.

The effects have since reached far beyond Tiananmen Square. The world stood by as Tibet was crushed and left to languish. The world stayed silent in the face of mounting evidence of forced organ harvesting. The same silence has greeted the Uyghur genocide, another atrocity rationalized or ignored for the sake of economic convenience. And now, as the CCP escalates its persecution of House Church Christians, with its detention of Pastor Jin Mingri (also known as Ezra Jin) and dozens of other leaders from Beijing's Zion Church in October 2025, I fear the same silence will prevail—though there are some initial positive signs, with this, alongside the Trump administration's response to the CCP's persecution of Catholic Jimmy Lai, being the strongest US government response to the CCP's persecution of Christians in memory.

THE DEFINING PATTERN

This has become the defining pattern ever since: the United States, under the pretext "spreading democracy," is lured into a trap of its own making while China patiently constructs an enormous system of economic leverage. Over time, the CCP came to hold many critical economic levers, which the Party can pull at will.

It is not an exaggeration to say that today, Beijing can choke off the supply of key materials, technologies, or markets almost at its discretion. And America's dependence has grown so deep that the cost of resistance—the cost of "poking the bear," so to speak—is now prohibitively high for far too many people in positions of power.

We are boxed in, and the way out is murky at best.

In retrospect, the CCP's approach was simple: get itself embedded in as many critical areas as possible, until it becomes almost impossible to pull them out. And then, when it no longer needs the West for a resource or a product, having extracted all the wealth and intellectual property possible, strategically decouple that area on the CCP's terms, or weaponize it. This has been an incredibly effective strategy—unrestricted warfare in slow motion.

The sheer range of goods, services, technologies, and resources on which the United States now relies on China is staggering—and should terrify anyone paying attention.

Take rare earths, for example, a market that China understood long before we did and cornered years ago. They control the manufacturing, the processing, the relationships—and the United States needs those materials for everything from advanced electronics to weapons systems. That gives the CCP real leverage.

In late 2025, Beijing pulled the trigger, demonstrating this dominance in a calculated escalation that served as a rude awakening for the West. It began on October 9, when China's Ministry of Commerce announced Announcement No. 61, imposing the strictest-ever export controls on rare earth elements, processing technologies, and permanent magnets—critical for US defense systems, electric vehicles, and semiconductors—in direct response to US chip bans and tariffs. Prices surged globally, with elements like dysprosium and terbium spiking as supply fears gripped markets, disrupting industries from Apple to Lockheed Martin. Step-by-step, the CCP showcased its chokehold: first, by withholding key exports to the United States, forcing stockpiling and emergency sourcing; second, by delaying enforcement on some items like holmium for a year in November amid a fragile trade truce, reminding everyone of its discretionary power; and third, by suspending certain curbs on lithium batteries and other minerals, but only after the point was made—China controls 85–90 percent of global rare earth processing, and it can weaponize that at will. This maneuver exposed America's vulnerabilities, sparking urgent calls for re-shoring and friend-shoring US supply chains. US new technologies like Rice University professor of materials science and nanotechnology James Tour's "Flash Joule Heating," which enables the extraction of rare earths, critical minerals and precious metals from electronic waste, cheaply, cleanly and at scale, offer perhaps the most immediate solution to rare earth dependence on the CCP, but as I write, policymakers have not yet fully jolted into action.[3]

The same holds true for our medical supply chains, which are completely entangled with China's manufacturing base and, essentially held hostage by the CCPs. That became painfully clear during COVID, when Beijing withheld medical supplies, turning a global health crisis into a geopolitical weapon. Per AP, a May 2020 US Department of Homeland Security (DHS) analysis marked "for official use only" concluded that, while intentionally downplaying the outbreak's severity, China ramped up imports of medical supplies and sharply curtailed its exports. The report further assessed that Beijing sought to conceal these moves by publicly denying any export restrictions and by delaying or obscuring the release of its trade data.[4]

The medical dependencies run far deeper, and the implications are no less terrifying. Rosemary Gibson, author of *China Rx*, and a national authority on health care policy and patient safety and senior advisor at the Hastings Center, who has testified before Congress on pharmaceutical supply chain vulnerabilities, told me in 2025 that "the United States depends on China for 95 percent of the key components that are necessary to make our generic drugs, and if China shut the door on exports, within months, our health care system would begin to collapse." President Trump has made efforts to move pharmaceutical manufacturing back to the United States, but the industry is resistant to reshoring for obvious reasons. China has almost no real regulatory oversight and runs almost entirely on graft. The crazy thing, as Gibson recounted, is that regulatory oversight for quality by the FDA when it comes to foreign generic drugs often functions, in essence, as a rubber stamp, compared to much more serious oversight at home. "How come we don't know that our medicines are being made in China? And this has been going on for a long time, and for years, there was actually zero regulation. How do we outsource production from a country with the highest standards in the world to places with no standards?" It's a much better place to do the kind of business they have gotten used to doing. In China, if you pay off the right people, a factory manager can dump toxic waste into a river with virtually no risk of fines, penalties, or even questions. It's cheaper, faster, and dirtier, and it lays bare how little regard the regime has for human life, even its own citizens. Entire communities live with the consequences: poisoned water, polluted air, and an ecosystem slowly destroyed by industrial runoff.

The American or multinational companies themselves may not even know what's happening—because they know better than to ask. Plausible deniability—or willful ignorance—is the name of the game. In that sense, American businesses can sometimes operate much like the CCP itself: they set the goal or strategic direction, and the lower levels of the system figure out how to achieve it, whatever it takes.

There have even been numerous documented cases where adulterated drugs and other life-sustaining products made it into the global markets—accidentally, perhaps, but proof of just how easy it would be to use the supply chain as a weapon. In one case, a manufacturer substituted a chemical that was designed to look like the real ingredient—but it wasn't the same. The result was catastrophic: people became very sick. The story broke widely because a prominent doctor himself checked into a hospital with massive heart failure after taking the adulterated product. This was the 2018 valsartan contamination scandal, where Chinese pharmaceutical giant Zhejiang Huahai Pharmaceutical produced the blood pressure and heart failure drug with a toxic impurity called N-nitrosodimethylamine (NDMA), a probable human carcinogen, due to changes in manufacturing processes. The adulterated valsartan, distributed globally through major companies like Novartis and Teva, led to widespread recalls affecting millions of patients in over thirty countries, with reports of severe allergic reactions, kidney damage, and at least eighty-one deaths linked to similar heparin contaminations from China in 2008. A Johns Hopkins-trained physician's near-fatal heart failure from the tainted medication highlighted the crisis, exposing how cost-cutting substitutions in China's supply chain endangered lives and underscoring vulnerabilities in global drug safety.

Back in 2020, when we first met, Gibson told me the following:

> The United States and the rest of the world are dramatically dependent on China for thousands of medicines that are taken every day. These are mostly generic drugs. And if China shuts the door on exports of the core chemicals and other ingredients to make them, we'll see the countries waiting in line to get vital medicines to care for their populations. We're already beginning to see the pricing rivalry for certain drugs that are becoming more scarce because global demand has increased with the coronavirus. It's a very serious situation that we're approaching. . . . We have a perfect storm. Production shutdowns have taken place in China because of the coronavirus. Workers were not going to work so they could stay home and take care of themselves and their families. Transportation routes have

> been constrained; there's a huge demand [for medicine] in China. And then, as the coronavirus spread around the world, global demand increased. Meanwhile, the whole supply chain for the world's medicines is concentrated in a single country. And now we're beginning to see countries like the United Kingdom, India, and even Hungary, as well as others, that are banning the exports of medicines, because they want to make sure that they have enough for their own people. These are unprecedented times that we're in. We're in uncharted waters.

But this was not enough to bring those supply chains back to America in a meaningful way. There are also reports that agencies such as the UN and the Department of Defense have been testing stockpiled drugs, finding a worrying share that don't meet acceptable specifications. As I write, Rosemary Gibson is telling me that US Antibiotics, the last US manufacturer of amoxicillin, and other US producers of critical medicines, are bypassed in government contracts to supply generics to the Department of War, VA, and HHS, losing to overseas producers too often selling substandard products from India, China, and other countries at firesale prices. She tells me that if US companies could be paid as little as an additional 25 cents per bottle, some could be financially viable. This would also provide a greater assurance of quality. Ironically, as I just mentioned, when it comes to generic drugs, domestic producers face more rigorous FDA scrutiny than foreign manufacturers with poor quality track records.

Now imagine that as an unrestricted-warfare tactic: low-quality or adulterated product shipped deliberately or negligently, targeted at populations that rely on it. People get sick, deaths mount, and tracing the cause takes time. From a cold strategic calculus, that's "win" after "win." From a human perspective, it's horrifying.

And that's just one of hundreds of possible attack vectors the CCP could exploit if it wanted to cause chaos.

That's the true danger of our dependence on China, which we've been running headlong into for the better part of three decades. It's not just about economics—who is making money, who is saving money, who is getting rich—it's about control. At the end of the day, when your enemy makes the things you need to survive—let alone fight—they don't have to fire a shot to win the war.

THE GREATEST DANGER

But in the end, the greatest danger the United States faces isn't simply the Chinese Communist Party's aggression, which may or may not rear its head sometime soon. Rather, it's our own blindness to what the CCP truly is and truly wants. For half a century, we've chosen to see the CCP not as a totalitarian system bent on domination, but as a misunderstood partner on the verge of reform—or at least susceptible to reform from the inside. We believed that trade would make China freer, that engagement would make the Party more like us. It was a comforting fiction—one that allowed us to justify looking away as our industries were hollowed out, our supply chains captured, and our institutions quietly infiltrated. What we misguidedly called globalization, they understood as a battlefield in unrestricted warfare—a method of conquest without bombs or armies, achieved through dependency, co-option, and moral compromise.

Nowhere is that compromise clearer than in medicine. The same ethical blindness that once justified our financial partnership with the CCP has, over time, dulled our moral sense of the value of human life itself. We have built research partnerships, hospital exchanges, and academic collaborations with a regime where organ procurement by murder is standard practice. In doing so, we've not only financed a crime against humanity—we've begun to absorb its logic, which, of course, has been the CCP's strategy all along. Chinese elites can be trusted to protect the system that guarantees them a steady supply of organs. But what happens when American elites become ensnared in that same system—when they, too, have a stake in keeping it alive?

The question we face now is not just how to contain China's influence, but how to recover our own moral clarity—to remember that prosperity without conscience, and science without humanity, are the surest ways to lose not only a war, but our soul.

CHAPTER 13

OPPORTUNITY FOR PEOPLE IN CHINA?

ENGAGEMENT HAS FAILED—NOW WHAT?

It's clear that Kissinger's blueprint has failed to live up to its promise. China is wealthier, yes, but the CCP is also more efficiently repressive with new technologies, more stridently ideological, more openly aggressive toward its adversaries, and more willing than ever to leverage its dominance in the global economy to achieve its aims.

So what can be done? And more importantly, what can the Chinese people—those living under the regime's shadow—do for themselves?

The truth, as we've discussed, is that there are few good ways to effect meaningful change inside a totalitarian system. Such regimes are designed precisely to prevent the natural, organic forces of civil society—the communities, associations, and institutions that make real reform possible—from emerging in the first place.

The CCP's prime directive—always—is its own survival, which it safeguards through the relentless pursuit of what it calls "social stability." The Party's unspoken contract with the people is simple: as long as it can deliver prosperity, even if that prosperity is corrupt, unsustainable, or built on illusion, the population will remain docile and compliant. So far, that strategy has worked, although cracks are increasingly appearing in the facade as China's export-driven economy falters.

But hearts and minds can and do change. And as they do, the Party's foundation weakens. Built as it is on smoke and mirrors, that same foundation could one day become the quicksand that pulls the CCP down. That is the hope for China, and the world.

TUI DANG, OR "QUITTING THE CCP"

The Tui Dang movement, an underground effort over the past two decades to encourage Chinese people to quit the Communist Party, was built on this very hope.[1]

The movement traces its roots to *The Nine Commentaries on the Communist Party*, written in 2004 by Chinese editors at *The Epoch Times*.[2] At the time, they were struggling to understand why the Party was behaving as it was—why it was persecuting Falun Gong and repressing dissent so ruthlessly. Drawing on deep historical research and personal experience, they produced what was, in effect, the first comprehensive history of Chinese communism written by Chinese people themselves. Previous works, such as "The Black Book of Communism," were excellent, but none spoke from inside the lived experience of communism "with Chinese characteristics." The *Nine Commentaries* really struck a nerve. It quickly became the most banned and hated (and for others, a "must read") book in China, a fiery indictment of the CCP's crimes and a searing exploration of its ideology, using the persecution of Falun Gong as one of its central examples. The book inspired the Tui Dang (退黨)—or "Quit the CCP"—movement, which began the same year, and took shape inspired by Falun Gong's principles of truthfulness, compassion, and forbearance.

Also known as the "Three Withdrawals" or "San Tui" (三退), it is a grassroots, non-violent initiative. It enables Chinese individuals worldwide to symbolically renounce their affiliations with the Chinese Communist Party (CCP) and its subordinate organizations—the Communist Youth League (CYL) and the Young Pioneers—through personal declarations. This act annuls the oaths of lifelong loyalty and self-sacrifice that nearly all Chinese citizens are coerced into making during childhood or as adults, often as a condition of education, employment, or social participation, says Caylan Ford, a Canadian writer, documentary filmmaker, and educator, who has extensively discussed the Tui Dang movement in her writings, as well as with me directly.

The movement asks for no public declarations, no grand gestures. Those who wish to renounce the Party may do so anonymously, through an encrypted database that records their decision. Over the past twenty years, activists have quietly encouraged millions—one person at a time—to make that choice.

For many, quitting the Party is a profoundly personal act, a way of letting go of fear and reclaiming one's moral agency. In a system that demands total allegiance, even performative allegiance, Tui Dang offers a quiet but radical alternative: to simply say, "I would rather live in a world without this. I would rather live in a normal society." Ford highlights how Tui Dang declarations serve as a moral and spiritual severance from the CCP's "gnostic cult-like" ideology, which she describes as a totalitarian force that demands total allegiance and suppresses transcendence. She notes US congressional resolutions (e.g., House Resolution 932 in 2016) expressing solidarity with Tui Dang, viewing it as a path to "reclaim Chinese history and culture" and foster a free society.

The vast, vast majority of the citizens of the People's Republic of China have at some point been members of at least one the CCP, the CYL, and the Young Pioneers—the exception being some very elderly people, born in the 1950's or earlier. So almost everyone is a candidate for quitting the Party and its affiliated organizations. At the time of writing, there exists a nucleus of over 455 million Chinese people who, by participating in Tui Dang, have separated themselves from the Party's grip on their soul—and counting. Not publicly, not loudly, not even empirically (I can't independently verify the numbers, as the owners of the database guard it with their lives, knowing full well what the CCP is capable of)—but meaningfully. It is an extraordinary movement, built on immense courage and the quiet conviction that freedom begins in the mind.

LIFE UNDER THE CCP

The people leaving the Party are doing so for any number of reasons. Some of it is simply looking honestly at history, which was one of the central goals of *The Nine Commentaries*. The book laid bare the hell the CCP created for the Chinese people.

There's a widespread perception, both in China and abroad, that the Party "lifted millions out of poverty," and in a narrow sense that's true. But what's rarely acknowledged is that the CCP created that level of poverty in the first place. The Great Leap Forward, collectivization, and decades of ideological campaigns left people so destitute that they were literally cannibalizing their children. So yes, they raised people from that level, but only after having driven them there.

It's a kind of national Stockholm Syndrome. The same regime that caused the suffering loosens its grip just enough to let people breathe—and demands gratitude for the relief. It's understandable, but it's not something to celebrate.

Others come to reject the Party for more personal reasons. They realize how stifling it is to live in a system where even the basics of human life—dignity, faith, freedom—are conditional. Some of them trust the people reaching out to them enough to say, "You know what, you're right. I don't want to live this way anymore." They take the risk, hoping it's not another "Hundred Flowers" moment—when Mao encouraged dissent, only to round up and kill those who spoke out.

The inequality in China today is staggering. Vice President JD Vance once used the term "peasant" to describe the Chinese working class, and it's not far off. In an April 3, 2025, interview on *Fox & Friends*, Vance critiqued the "globalist economy" by explaining that it relies on two flawed pillars: massive US debt to finance imports from China, and outsourcing jobs to Chinese workers who then hold the bonds for that debt.[3] "To make it a little more crystal clear," he said, "we borrow money from Chinese peasants to buy the things those Chinese peasants manufacture." The remark, made while defending Trump administration tariffs, drew sharp backlash from Beijing, which called it "ignorant and impolite," and sparked viral rebuttals on Chinese social media touting the nation's high-speed rail, AI advancements, and logistics prowess as proof of its modernity. But even the CCP itself sometimes uses the word. For most ordinary people, life is harsh. Migrant workers move constantly to find work. Factory conditions are brutal—so much so that suicide nets hang outside dormitories. Health outcomes are poor, property ownership is out of reach, and millions live in what amounts to modern slave labor.

And that's the great myth of the "Chinese market." There is no true market. The idea that China could become a genuine consumer society was always a fiction. The system is designed to serve the Party, not the people. Workers save what little they can, but those savings are funneled into state banks—used to buy US debt and manipulate currency rather than improve their own lives. Vice President Vance described this dynamic vividly, pointing out how it affects nearly half a billion people who live perpetually on the edge.

For the elite, of course, it's a different world entirely: Bentleys, yachts, and luxury homes in Beijing, Shanghai, and abroad. But that group is vanishingly small. For everyone else, the promise of prosperity remains mostly out of reach—a mirage sustained by propaganda, fear, and the faint hope that things might somehow get better.

There used to be a group just below the elites—a kind of middle class—but that middle class has been shrinking fast. The CCP has repeatedly printed and pumped money that doesn't really exist into the economy, inflating away people's savings and hollowing out their purchasing power.

Much of this middle class had poured its wealth into real estate. Property ownership was seen as the safest, most reliable way to secure one's future—almost a sacred promise of prosperity. But that promise collapsed when the property sector imploded after 2021: the CCP's sudden debt crackdown (the "three red lines" policy) forced developers like Evergrande into default, freezing construction on millions of pre-sold apartments and instantly erasing trillions in household wealth.[4] It was a *massive* bubble. Tens of millions of ordinary buyers—who had paid in full upfront, often borrowing from relatives—are now stuck with unfinished homes they cannot live in and mortgages they still must pay, while property values have fallen 20-40 percent in many cities. With real estate once accounting for roughly 70 percent of Chinese household assets and a quarter of GDP, the crash has delivered a body blow to middle-class security that the regime has no realistic plan to reverse.

You can grow GDP the right way, by making things people actually use. Or you can do it the CCP way: through "make-work" projects, construction for construction's sake. That's what they did, building entire empty cities to hit growth targets.

The problem with this kind of central planning—this top-down social engineering that the CCP loves—is that it creates enormous second-order effects that no one bothers to predict.

They dictate a goal from the top, issue the directive—"make it happen by any means necessary"—and leave the rest to the bureaucracy. The result? Unintended consequences on a national scale.

For years, people believed that investing in property was as close to a guaranteed win as you could get. After all, the state was always right, always benevolent, always in control—at least, that's what they were taught. In reality, those guarantees never existed. Corruption, kickbacks, and local graft infected every layer of the system, and when the property market collapsed, it took with it the life savings of hundreds of millions.

That's what happened to the middle class. It's been wiped out, its savings destroyed by inflation, its investments evaporated in the property collapse, and its confidence shattered. What remains is a society that's aging rapidly, with too many men and not enough women, and a dangerous imbalance between rich and poor.

For everyone unlucky enough to be born outside the upper echelon of Chinese society, given the harsh realities of life and the ever-tightening grip of Party control, I find the Tui Dang movement to be the most interesting, and in many ways, the most compelling challenge to the regime. What makes it remarkable is that its participants aren't seeking to overthrow the CCP or spark revolution; they are simply choosing, quietly, to withdraw their consent.

Yet, should the regime fall—and it's always in danger of doing so, given its parasitic nature and the corruption that sustains it—there now exists a core of people ready to take on the work of rebuilding a normal society. In recent years, the CCP has lost major pillars of its economy and is increasingly dependent on exports and state manipulation to stay afloat. The foundation is cracking, even if the structure still stands.

Unfortunately, genuine reform from within is almost impossible. The Party's survival instinct is to destroy anything independent—any thought, belief, or organization that isn't under its control. Those are precisely the things that could help it evolve, but its nature won't allow it.

You can't "totalitarian" your way out of totalitarianism.

CHAPTER 14

LEGISLATING AGAINST EVIL

A GROWING AWARENESS

We're living in an unprecedented time—one defined by a growing awareness not only of forced organ harvesting, but of the CCP's broader ambitions for global dominance and the methods they use toward that goal.

Over the past several years, particularly since the pandemic, the mask has slipped, and the world has gotten a rare glimpse of what the CCP is truly capable of. The COVID-19 virus itself may have been a weapon developed, or at least exploited, by the Party. Many people believe the virus was released intentionally to create chaos. It's an unsettling theory—but the very fact that it sounds plausible tells us something about how far the Party is willing to go. In any normal society, such an idea would seem outrageous. In the context of the CCP, it's disturbingly reasonable.

Whether the virus was leaked deliberately or not, the fact remains: they seized the opportunity. The CCP used the crisis to scuttle major trade negotiations, to consolidate power internally, and to take over Hong Kong—a place that had once stood as one of the freest and most economically open societies in the world. That Hong Kong is gone. Everyone knows it. And today, anyone who speaks out against the regime can face years in prison, even those living abroad. It was a massive shift in strategy, executed almost in plain sight.

The world also saw the Party's true face: the PPE blackmail, the manipulation of air travel, the citizens being welded into their homes. It was a chilling demonstration of what totalitarian "efficiency" looks like. And we have to ask ourselves: Is that the kind of efficiency we want here?

There's a growing recognition now, across many fronts, that this is a far bigger problem than anyone once imagined. Not everyone sees it, of course. Some still push propaganda, showing videos of "dancing Uyghurs" and carefully curated images of harmony. But overall, there's a shift. No serious observer still believes China is "almost democratic." That illusion is gone.

This awareness is beginning to translate into real-world action. The US Commission on International Religious Freedom, the State Department, the CECC, and numerous human rights groups have documented the atrocities.[1] There's widespread acknowledgment that the CCP's treatment of Uyghurs amounts to genocide. And, finally, after decades of silence, the issue of forced organ harvesting is gaining traction.

It might seem modest compared to the scale of the crime, but to those of us who have watched this for twenty years, it's an enormous change. The arrival of a living survivor—someone who can testify from experience—has transformed the conversation. For the first time, it's becoming impossible to look away. Multiple experts, including former US Assistant Secretary of State for Democracy, Human Rights, and Labor Robert Destro and former US Ambassador-at-Large for International Religious Freedom Sam Brownback, agree with me that the CCP is in fact engaging in three genocides: the brutal suppression and forced assimilation of the Uyghur Muslim population in Xinjiang, the systematic cultural erasure and demographic swamping of Tibetan Buddhists, and the cold genocide against Falun Gong with forced organ harvesting as its key pillar.

And the collective consciousness around the CCP's large scale forced organ harvesting from prisoners of conscience has really started to shift. People are opening their eyes. Kash Patel, a few months before being nominated for FBI Director, had me on an episode of *War Room* to tell Cheng Pei Ming's survivor story. The episode went viral across multiple platforms, and I experienced a flurry of interest in the subject that I had never experienced before. I thought, people might finally be ready to accept this is real! But the nuclear bomb of awareness that went off a few months later when Mike Rowe of *Dirty Jobs* fame had me on his podcast *The Way I Heard It* was something that I frankly wasn't ready for.[2] The long-form episode, titled "Is This Really Happening in China?" went super-viral and played a pivotal role in seeing this book realized.[3] Hundreds of people, including prominent medical professionals, government officials, and media practitioners and publishers, reached out, asking, what can I do?

This attention must be seized upon.

If there's ever been a moment when truth could break through the machinery of denial, this is it. It could be game-changing, not just for how the world sees the CCP, but for how we choose to respond to it.

The first sign of real progress is at the state level. Six states have already enacted laws addressing forced organ harvesting, with several others in progress. Texas was the first; the most recent is Arkansas. Arizona's bill initially failed but was later reintroduced and passed.

These laws broadly prohibit state-regulated health insurance plans, state employee benefits, and state Medicaid programs from covering or reimbursing organ transplants performed in China, while also banning the use of organs known or suspected to have been sourced through forced harvesting. It's a moral and financial line in the sand—a statement that we will not, even indirectly, subsidize murder for profit.

Any state can take up this model legislation. Six have done it already.

The question is: Why not fifty?

At the federal level, as I write, there are now three laws in play. One, the Block Organ Transplant Purchases from China Act, mirrors the state-level legislation I mentioned above and is currently being considered in US House committee.

The other two have already passed the House, nearly unanimously, in the 119th United States Congress. One is the Falun Gong Protection Act, led by Congressmen Scott Perry and Patrick Ryan in the House, which passed without any dissent at all. Its companion bill is led in the Senate by Senator Ted Cruz, having picked it up from now Secretary of State Marco Rubio. The other is the Stop Forced Organ Harvesting Act, introduced in the House by Congressmen Chris Smith and Bill Keating. It doesn't yet have a companion bill in the Senate, though in the previous congress it was sponsored by Senators Tom Cotton and Chris Coons. Both are strong, necessary pieces of legislation.

The Falun Gong Protection Act is narrowly focused on China, and that's important. China should be identified as a particular problem, even as broader legislation addresses organ harvesting globally. Naming Falun Gong explicitly as a persecuted group would be especially meaningful, as this has not happened yet in US legislation. Still, both bills represent real progress, and both stand a genuine chance of becoming law.

All this is an opportunity—to advance legislation at every level of government, to raise public awareness, and to apply meaningful pressure that could help stop these crimes. Even at a minimum, these bills serve a vital purpose: they force acknowledgment. Awareness creates accountability, and accountability drives change.

The proposed federal laws would also sanction Chinese elites directly involved in the organ-harvesting system. That's significant because every Chinese elite has an exit strategy—usually to the United States or another free country or one with no extradition treaty. They know China's political landscape is unstable, fractured by rivalries and factional infighting. When things go wrong, they need somewhere safe to flee.

Sanctions change that calculus. If you're sanctioned, your escape route—your US investments, your real estate, your foreign passports—suddenly becomes a liability. That, in turn, can make participation in these crimes far less attractive.

It's far from a complete solution, but it's a start. At least a few people, those who are really intent on their exit strategies, will steer clear of being in any way associated with the forced organ harvesting system. And that will save a few lives. A very meaningful few.

It also sends a clear, unambiguous message: We see what you're doing. We know it's happening. And it's wrong.

For a long time, progress on this issue was glacial—measured in inches, not miles. But for the first time in decades, it feels like genuine movement.

There's also a tremendous amount that can be done at the institutional level.

We should start by asking a basic question: In how many ways does the US transplant system currently interact with China's? The list is long. There's the training of transplant professionals, often through programs funded by the Department of Health and Human Services (HHS) or by US institutions themselves. There are hospital partnerships, medical school and university collaborations, research grants, teaching exchanges, and even joint initiatives supported by HHS and the National Institutes of Health (NIH).

Then there's the matter of transplant technology and materials—a massive area of cooperation that few people fully grasp.

One legislative option that hasn't yet been considered could be modelled after the Wolf Amendment. As I wrote in the *Baltimore Sun* op-ed I mentioned earlier, it restricts NASA's cooperation with China to protect sensitive technologies.[4] A similar law could bar US health agencies, universities, hospitals and companies from working with Chinese transplant entities unless they can prove ethical sourcing.

The good news is that some progress is possible on the US agency front, too. There's a growing group of people, including within HHS leadership, who genuinely want to address this issue. The HHS official X account, in September of 2025, declared, "In China, forced organ harvesting of prisoners has continued for over twenty years. To affirm the sanctity of human life, America must sever its ties with China's organ transplant system." Speaking with HHS officials directly, I've been able to verify that their interest is serious, and growing.

HHS Secretary Kennedy's recent domestic reforms to organ procurement, in fact, offer a model for action.[5] HHS imposed penalties on an American organ procurement organization after finding that 29 percent of its cases showed "concerning features." It also instituted wider reforms like mandatory patient safety officers, enhanced monitoring and zero tolerance for violations. These should extend to international partnerships as well.

For example, the United States could stop enabling China's industrial-scale violations. Of course, HHS has no jurisdiction over China, but it can ensure American entities aren't involved through the lever of funding, similar to how the Trump administration recently terminated $2 billion in grants to Harvard for civil rights violations and policy misalignment.

No American institution should collaborate with Chinese transplant programs until forced organ harvesting ends. No NIH grant should support research involving Chinese transplant centers or personnel.

There are also more out-of-the-box legal approaches, like the one proposed by law professor Joanmarie Ilaria Davoli. Davoli argues in her January 2025 SSRN paper "Harvesting Humans" that federal statute 18 U.S.C. §956 could be used to prosecute Americans involved in organ tourism or transplant arrangements tied to forced organ harvesting abroad.[6] It's a creative interpretation, but a sound one. The statute makes it a crime for US citizens to conspire to kidnap, maim, or kill a person in a foreign country—and that is, in essence, what's happening when someone knowingly participates in a system built on murder for organs.

It's an avant-garde legal theory, but one that makes moral and logical sense. More importantly, it could serve as a powerful deterrent—sending the message that Americans who take part in these atrocities, even indirectly, will be held accountable under US law.

A GRASSROOTS MOVEMENT

But perhaps the only real force capable of overcoming Chinese money and influence is a grassroots movement—ordinary people demanding that their leaders act. That's the key.

Because this isn't the kind of legislation anyone can openly oppose. No one wants to be the person arguing against stopping forced organ harvesting. That's why these bills keep passing the House with overwhelming, near-unanimous support. Take the Falun Gong Protection Act—it passed without a single dissent. That says something, in a Congress where it's not so common to see Republicans and Democrats agree by consensus.

Forced organ harvesting is one of those moral issues you simply can't defend publicly. The only way to stop these bills is quietly—by letting them die in committee, getting them edited out of a larger package, or stalling them procedurally. No one can stand up on the floor of Congress and say, "I'm against this," without looking like a monster.

That's why a genuine, bottom-up push could make all the difference. Call your senator. Get your friends to call theirs. Organize small groups, write letters, post about it. Senators do count phone calls—I know that for a fact.

To further help at the grassroots level, Rotary Club members have stepped up, creating an "End Forced Organ Harvesting Rotary Satellite Club," and they've gotten busy helping people organize screenings of the recent Oscar-nominated film, *State Organs: Unmasking Transplant Abuse in China* and expert panels at local libraries and community centers, to raise awareness. Get involved![7]

This is one of those rare cases where the public can actually outweigh the lobbyists and the money. If enough people speak up—if voters in a state make it clear that this issue matters—it can move the needle. It really can.

EPILOGUE

IT'S NOT TOO LATE

THE CCP VS. THE CHINESE PEOPLE

Let me be clear: this book is not anti-China.

The Chinese people are incredibly resourceful. It's a magnificent culture—one of the world's oldest and most sophisticated. And this is something that must be made absolutely clear: this is a pro-China book. The Party, the persecution, the killing—those are not the true nature of China. Traditional Chinese culture is deeply spiritual, compassionate, and, perhaps surprisingly, places great value on the individual.

We've been taught to think that Chinese civilization—because of communism, or even because of its imperial past—treats people like ants. But that's not true. It's far more nuanced. There were dynasties, such as the Tang, that embodied openness, freedom of faith, and extraordinary cultural and intellectual flourishing. That era is still considered the height of Chinese civilization.

The acts described in this book—the atrocities, the manipulation, the repression—I hope you now realize how deeply antihumanity, and as such, anti-China, they really are. The crimes of the Chinese Communist Party are crimes against China itself.

This, in fact, may be the most powerful act of ideological warfare the CCP has ever waged: convincing both the Chinese people and the world that China and the Party are the same thing. That illusion allows the regime to use the Chinese people as both shield and sword, exploiting them at will to preserve its own survival.

But it isn't true. The Chinese people are not the Party.

They are, and always have been, the Party's greatest victims.

IT'S ALREADY HAPPENING HERE, BUT IT'S NOT TOO LATE

The issues discussed in this book extend far beyond what happens in China, and it's imperative that we recognize how they are already eroding our moral framework right here at home.

There are now two countries where medically assisted suicide is formally recognized and performed as a medical treatment—Canada and the Netherlands. Both have created a billing code for suicide. Once that happens, implementation accelerates rapidly. In Canada, for instance, in 2023, medically assisted death was the fifth leading cause of death, behind cancer, heart disease, COVID-19, and accidents, but ahead of cerebrovascular diseases and chronic respiratory issues.[1] The transplant system, naturally, is interested in these patients, many of whom are otherwise healthy in ways that make them ideal organ donors. And you can easily imagine where this goes next. As eligibility expands to mental illness (slated to happen in 2027 in Canada), what happens when someone asks, "Can I offer you death as a solution to your depression?" If you're socially isolated or struggling, and someone tells you your organs could save a life, that can sound almost noble.

This is already galloping ahead in Canada, spreading quietly in parts of the United States, and deeply entrenched in places like the Netherlands, where roughly sixty thousand people have now been euthanized by doctors.

The danger isn't just the act itself. The issue is also how it softens our ethics. *The New York Times* recently ran an op-ed by three physicians arguing that we should loosen the dead-donor rule—the basic requirement that a person must be declared dead before their organs can be removed.[2] That's the exact logic of CCP-style utilitarian bioethics creeping into our own system: that the end justifies the means, that killing can be rationalized if it serves a "greater good."[3]

The closer we move toward accepting that premise, the more vulnerable we become to the same moral compromises that define the CCP's approach.

A doctor recently described a horrifying development to me: some physicians, in his experience, were becoming far too quick to declare brain death than in the past. HHS investigations revealed twenty-eight cases where American patients "may not have been truly deceased when the organ procurement process began."[4] That's when you realize it's not just about isolated cases—it's a mentality. A culture of thinking.

And that's the most dangerous part: this mentality of social engineering, the belief that it's acceptable to break a few eggs for the greater good. Once you start making moral trade-offs—deciding whether to err on the side of life or to proceed because there's an 80 percent chance the patient is gone—you've already stepped outside Hippocratic medicine and into utilitarian medicine, which only moves in one direction. And it moves fast.

We must draw the line clearly: people must truly be dead before organs are harvested—otherwise, we are crossing into killing.

This isn't theoretical; it's all there in the journals. It starts as a "thought experiment," and before long, it quietly becomes policy, a phenomenon documented by Wesley Smith in his seminal book, *Culture of Death*, chronicling the rise of utilitarian bioethics in free societies.[5]

By normalizing these ideas, we internalize them. If you're

working with Chinese transplant surgeons, you're working with murderers. That's their normal. They kill people as often as they perform surgeries. And what does that do to you? You rationalize it. You tell yourself you're saving lives, or that reform is coming, or that you're not personally responsible. Because human beings have an unlimited capacity for rationalization.

That's why we must have strict ethical boundaries. The idea of loosening the dead donor rule is a disaster waiting to happen. Once you loosen it, you can't go back. It's the ratchet effect again—each click pushing the boundary further until the principle itself disappears.

We need to understand what's truly at stake.

This isn't just about what's happening in China, or even the global reach of the Chinese Communist Party—it's about how we are being changed. Each compromise, each rationalization, moves us closer to the same materialist, dignity-free worldview that underpins communism itself.

That's the endgame: not just to dominate us, but to make us think like them, and to shift our moral horizon incrementally until our shared values are indistinguishable from Party aims, until even our freedom, our bodies, and our souls become just more instruments of the Party's survival.

APPENDIX 1

A SKEPTIC'S GUIDE TO THE EVIDENCE

I've heard every objection in the book, sometimes from people who genuinely want to believe the best about humanity, sometimes from those who, deep down, just don't want to know. That "desire not to know," as Solzhenitsyn put it, or what Orwell called "the will to disbelieve the horrible," has allowed this atrocity to continue far longer than it ever should have. But once you've looked at the evidence—the phone calls, the testimonies, the impossible numbers, the admissions—it becomes impossible to look away.

What follows are the most common questions I've been asked, the ones that let people stay comfortable a little longer. I answer them not to win an argument, but because lives are still being taken, right now, to order. The victims, mostly peaceful Falun Gong practitioners, and increasingly Uyghurs and others, deserve for us to face the truth squarely.

OBJECTION 1:
"It's just death-row prisoners who were already going to be executed anyway."

It is true that China's earliest experimentation began with prisoners sentenced to death, and some of the earliest admissions by doctors involved tell horrific stories of waiting in vans outside prison walls to be brought prisoners for organ removal. And pre-1999, when China's volume of transplants was very low, it is likely that most forced organ harvesting came from death row prisoners. However, Chinese officials denied this vehemently for decades. It was only after the evidence of the killing of huge numbers of imprisoned Falun Gong practitioners for organs began to emerge, that Chinese officials, in an attempt to deflect attention from that evidence, finally admitted in 2015 that executed prisoners had been the source of the majority of its transplant organs. On this point, it is important to note that Chinese officials claimed the executed criminals had "consented." But this itself is contrary to international transplant ethics. Consent under threat of death isn't consent. It's coercion.

The early connection between China's execution system and organ transplant field can help us understand how forced organ harvesting began, but death row prisoners can in no way account for the enormous transplant industry that grew in the early 2000s. Official execution numbers plummeted after 2007 to a few thousand a year, while transplant volumes skyrocketed. That growth can't be explained by death-row prisoners.

Only prisoners of conscience, especially Falun Gong practitioners and later Uyghurs, were subjected to systematic blood testing and organ examinations that ordinary criminals never received. Those tests weren't for their health; they were to tissue-type and organ-scan them for the transplant market. Hospital staff have admitted on recorded calls that healthy Falun Gong practitioners' organs were taken. The primary source isn't condemned criminals, it's innocent people killed on demand.

In a nutshell: Transplant numbers exploded while executions dropped. Only prisoners of conscience got the selective medical exams. Death-row prisoners can't account for the volume.

OBJECTION 2:
"The numbers are exaggerated. No way that many transplants happen."

They're not exaggerated; if anything, the estimates are conservative. Investigators used China's own official data—hospital beds, approved transplant centers, surgeon reports, massive hospital expansions. Individual hospitals openly reported hundreds or thousands of transplants annually. The estimates don't even include military hospitals because their transplant numbers are not publicly reported. Investigators still arrived at sixty thousand to ninety thousand transplants per year at peak.

In addition to calculating the estimates using China's own official data, there is evidence of a massive amount of readily available organs. Waiting times were days or weeks. Sometimes patients were offered multiple matching organs, something impossible in any legitimate system. With so many patients in need of transplant organs, so many people willing to pay, and such apparent ease in finding matching organs, of course there would be a large volume of transplant operations per year. The numbers aren't hype; they're the inescapable result of looking honestly at China's own records and the abundance of available organs.

In a nutshell: China's own data, conservatively analyzed, shows sixty thousand to ninety thousand transplants a year.

OBJECTION 3:
"Whatever happened in the past, the 2015 reforms ended it. Now it's all voluntary."

If only. China announced in 2015 that it would stop using executed prisoners and rely solely on voluntary donors. But transplant volumes didn't drop. They stayed high or rose. The official "voluntary" donation numbers follow a perfectly smooth mathematical curve, the kind you get from a formula, not from real human behavior. That's fabrication, plain and simple, and Matthew Robertson proved in a peer-reviewed paper. Senior officials like Huang Jiefu have admitted they simply re-labeled prisoner organs as "voluntary" to comply with the new rules.

Even if we were to believe China's official "voluntary" donations numbers, they still would not be able to account for its volume of annual organ transplants. In the US, with a massive number of organ donors, the wait for a matching transplant organ is still very long because only a tiny fraction of those donors will provide organs in a given year. Using China's own reported figures, their pool of "voluntary" organ donors would yield 200 percent more organs than the US or the UK. Some Chinese hospitals reported more transplants than their entire province had voluntary donors.

And the fact remains, independent reviews after 2015, including the 2020 China Tribunal, concluded the killing continues.

In a nutshell: No drop in volume after the "reforms." Donation numbers are mathematically fake and implausible. Investigators have confirmed the practice goes on.

OBJECTION 4:
"This is just anti-China propaganda pushed by Falun Gong."

This is the standard line the CCP uses, usually with much more colorful language. Early on, some reports, like the initial Sujiatun allegations, couldn't be fully verified, and skeptics seized on that to dismiss everything. The core findings come from independent investigators, most with no Falun Gong affiliation at all: David Kilgour and David Matas (a former Canadian MP and a human-rights lawyer), journalist Ethan Gutmann, academic Matthew Robertson, and the independent China Tribunal chaired by Sir Geoffrey Nice QC, the British prosecutor who put war criminals like Milošević on trial. Also, the idea that "Falun Gong affiliation" itself is somehow disqualifying is in fact misdirection and built on slander. *Of course* Falun Gong practitioners (who happen to have a core guiding virtue of Truthfulness) will be highly motivated to help figure out what's happening with respect to the Chinese regime's atrocities against them. And independent researchers assess their work. It makes a ton of sense to work this way.

Researchers used undercover phone calls to hospitals, survivor and eyewitness testimony from multiple sources, Chinese medical journals, hospital records, and data analysis. The China Tribunal concluded forced organ harvesting from prisoners of conscience was proven "beyond reasonable doubt." The evidence stands on its own.

In a nutshell: Independent lawyers, journalists, and an international Tribunal, all unaffiliated with Falun Gong, as well as efforts by Falun Gong practitioners themselves and affiliated entities, reached the same conclusion: it's real, and proven beyond reasonable doubt.

OBJECTION 5:
"The Chinese authorities flatly deny it."

The CCP's story has changed repeatedly. First they denied taking organs from prisoners at all. Then they admitted most came from executed prisoners. After 2015, they claimed everything was voluntary. Yet the "voluntary" numbers are clearly manufactured and even their interpretation of what "voluntary" means is questionable. The words of Chinese authorities don't hold up against the evidence. Waiting times remain impossibly short and recorded hospital admissions plus survivor testimonies directly contradict the official line.

Chinese authorities have also never provided any evidence to prove their denials. They have not provided international oversight bodies nor independent investigators access to review their organ sourcing data. At the foundation of transplant ethics is the transparency and traceability of donated organs. China has never provided a transparent or traceable look at their system.

In a nutshell: The official narrative has shifted multiple times, and the post-2015 "voluntary" numbers are fabricated. The evidence contradicts the denials.

OBJECTION 6:
"There's no hard proof. There are no bodies, no documents, just stories and guesses."

The crime scene is an operating room, scrubbed clear after each surgery. Bodies are cremated immediately after organ removal. That's standard procedure to destroy evidence. But the circumstantial case is overwhelming and consistent across sources: hospital staff admitting it on secret recordings; targeted medical testing of Falun Gong and Uyghur detainees that other prisoners don't receive; transplant volumes and short waiting times that defy explanation without a live donor pool; confessions and testimonies that align from completely separate witnesses. The independent China Tribunal reviewed it all and found the crime proven. And, on top of it all, there is, amazingly, a survivor, Cheng Pei Ming, missing part of his liver and part of his lung, and the Chinese regime admits to having operated on him without consent.

In a nutshell: The crime scene is an operating room, bodies are destroyed, but the recordings, testimonies, testing patterns, and impossible numbers form a mountain of evidence no honest investigator can dismiss. On top of that, there is the survivor, Cheng Pei Ming.

OBJECTION 7:
"Major medical organizations accept China's reforms."
Some transplant societies accepted China's claims at face value, perhaps due to wishful thinking, or eagerness to resume collaboration and training exchanges. But they didn't do their own independent investigations. When you dig into the data, including fabricated donation curves, no drops in volume and hospitals outperforming their supposed donor pools, the "reform" narrative collapses. The China Tribunal and other independent researchers found the evidence more than sufficient to conclude the crime continues.

In a nutshell: Some organizations took China's word without scrutiny. The data fraud and unchanged transplant volumes show the supposed 2015 reforms were cosmetic. Independent reviews prove it's still happening.

These answers draw directly from the foundational investigations: Kilgour-Matas-Gutmann reports, the China Tribunal Judgment, Ethan Gutmann's fieldwork, Matthew Robertson's research, and the Victims of Communism review. The evidence isn't perfect; no crime that's considered by the CCP to be a state secret, the revealing of which is punishable by death, can ever be. But it is more than enough. Knowing what we know, how can we keep looking away? The victims are still waiting for us to find the courage to act.

APPENDIX 2

WHAT WE CAN DO TO CONFRONT AND END FORCED ORGAN HARVESTING IN CHINA

The evidence laid out in these pages is stark and undeniable: A state-run industry in China is killing innocent people—mostly prisoners of conscience, especially Falun Gong practitioners and Uyghurs—on demand, to order, for their organs. This isn't a relic of some dark past; it's happening right now, sustained by a totalitarian system that erodes consciences, rewards sociopathy, and relies on lies to survive. We've seen this before in history, and we know the cost of willful blindness—of choosing "not to know." But if you find this book compelling, I believe you sense we no longer have that excuse. Silence in the face of such evil makes us complicit. Truth demands courage, and courage demands action. The actions below, pulled directly from the realities and momentum described in this book, are practical ways we can bear witness and help stop this atrocity.

ACTIONS FOR EVERY ONE OF US

- Refuse to stay silent: Share what you've learned here with family, friends, colleagues—anyone who will listen. Knowing and doing nothing is no longer an option when lives hang in the balance.
- Deepen your understanding and spread the word: Dive into the foundational reports—the Kilgour-Matas investigation, the independent China Tribunal judgment, the Victims of Communism review—and pass them on.
- Reach out to your representatives: Pick up the phone or send an email to your senators and House members. They really do track those calls and letters. Urge them to prioritize the bills pending right now.
- Build momentum together: Gather a small group, write op-eds or letters to editors, post thoughtfully online, share new articles from *The Epoch Times* and other media when they cover this, rally friends to join you. Numbers matter.
- Contact the End Forced Organ Harvesting Rotary Satellite Club about hosting a film screening or panel discussion at your local library or community center.[1] Feature films, available on major platforms:
    - » *Red Reign: The Bloody Harvest of China's Prisoners*, 2013, Masha Savitz
    - » *Human Harvest*, 2014, Leon Lee
    - » *Hard to Believe*, 2016, Ken Stone and Irene Silber
    - » *State Organs: Unmasking Transplant Abuse in China*, 2024, Raymond Zhang
- Contact your state medical association and ask them to take a position against China's forced organ harvesting.
- Sign the international joint DAFOH - ETAC petition.[2]
- If you're still not sure how to get involved and want ideas, or have a tip, or just want to tell us your thoughts about what you read in this book, please write me and my team

at killedtoorder@protonmail.com. And Protonmail-to-Protonmail email communications are highly encrypted and relatively secure, should you want that.

CHAMPION KEY FEDERAL LEGISLATION

- Press for approval of the **Falun Gong Protection Act (H.R. 1540 / S. 817)**: Targeted sanctions—visas blocked, assets frozen—for anyone directly tied to this forced harvesting, and government tracking of this atrocity. Also, this bill, despite being broader, names in its title, Falun Gong practitioners as a CCP-persecuted group for the first time.
- Support the **Stop Forced Organ Harvesting Act of 2025 (H.R. 1503)**. More broadly-targeted than the Falun Gong Protection Act (broader than China alone), it would sanction those involved, boost transparency and reporting, and curb exports of transplant-related devices.
- Advocate for the **Block Organ Transplant Purchases from China Act of 2025 (H.R. 2114, "BLOCK Act")**: Still in committee, this would bar federal funds (Medicare, Medicaid) from covering transplants sourced in China, shutting down any American complicity through transplant tourism.
- Call for bold new standalone legislation—directly modeled on the proven Wolf Amendment that prohibits any US federal agency, grantee, contractor, or funded entity from cooperating, sharing data, conducting joint research, training, selling materials or equipment, or engaging in any activities with China related to organ transplantation, drawing a firm moral and practical line against complicity in this crime.

STRENGTHEN PROTECTIONS AT THE STATE LEVEL

- Work to expand state laws banning insurance reimbursement or public funding for organ transplants linked to forced harvesting in China: Six states have already taken this vital stand—Texas, Arizona, Idaho, Tennessee, Utah, Arkansas—leaving forty-four more where we can make a real difference.

BROADER INSTITUTIONAL AND POLICY STEPS

- **End all cooperation with China's transplant system:** Extend restrictions, perhaps modeled after the Wolf Amendment, to block joint training, research, or data exchanges.
- **Use federal funding as leverage:** Condition HHS and NIH grants on strict ethical compliance, cutting ties to any tainted programs.
- **Pursue accountability here at home:** Back the application of US laws (like 18 U.S.C. § 956) to prosecute involvement in unethical organ tourism.
- Insist on global transparency: **Push for stronger monitoring, penalties, and ethical safeguards in all international transplant partnerships.**

This crime against humanity continues as we speak. But we've seen awareness grow into real change, and it starts with us. Over the last twenty-five years, Falun Gong practitioners, by interacting with one person at a time, have played a major role in changing people's thinking about the CCP. Just like them, we can do it, one voice, one call, one social media post, one letter at a time. How can we, knowing what we know, look away? The victims deserve our courage. Let's act.

ACKNOWLEDGMENTS

This book begins and ends with the victims: the countless prisoners of conscience in China, primarily Falun Gong practitioners, but also Uyghurs, and likely Tibetans, House Church Christians, and others whose organs were stolen while they were still alive, all to feed an industry built on murder for profit. To you, and to the families shattered by your loss, I dedicate these pages. Your suffering is unimaginable, yet your quiet dignity in the face of such evil has been a constant reminder of why this truth must be told. I hope this work honors your sacrifice and helps bring about the day when this atrocity finally ends.

None of us would even know about the Chinese Communist Party's forced organ harvesting industry without the pioneering work of a few extraordinarily brave people and organizations. David Kilgour (dear friend, I still feel the void you left) and David Matas, your 2006 report lit the first real light on this darkness when the world wanted nothing to do with it. Ethan Gutmann, your dogged investigations (and thank you for those intense, eye-opening conversations) pushed us further into the abyss than anyone thought possible. The dedicated investigators at WOIPFG (World Organization to Investigate the Persecution of Falun Gong), your relentless, often dangerous pursuit of evidence has uncovered truths that no one else could. Matthew Robertson, your meticulous analysis of the data and scientific papers has been indispensable. Prof. Dr. Wendy Rogers, your tireless work pushing forward transplant ethics and challenging the global medical community to confront this horror has been equally vital.

To the advocates who have kept the pressure on year after year: Dr. Torsten Trey, Dr. Andreas Weber, and the whole Doctor Against Forced Organ Harvesting (DAFOH) team; Susie Hughes and everyone at the International Coalition to End Transplant Abuse in China (ETAC); Sir Geoffrey Nice, Prof. Arthur Waldron, and the other members of the China Tribunal panel: your independent judgment in 2020 was a landmark that no one can ignore. Dr. Jacob Lavee, when confronted firsthand with the chilling reality of forced organ harvesting through one of your own patients who scheduled a transplant in China on a precise date, you chose to act—your courageous early stand as a transplant surgeon not only resonated through history but directly led to the passage of some of the first laws countering this atrocity.

The survivors who trusted me with their stories—Cheng Pei Ming, your account of what happened on that operating table still shakes me to my core; Enver Tohti, for revealing the horrors you were coerced into; and others who must remain nameless for their safety: your courage is what makes this book more than just mere words.

I'm forever grateful to those who gave this issue a platform when it was still radioactive: Konstantin Kisin and Francis Foster on Triggernometry, Kash Patel filling in on *War Room*, Steve Bannon, Mike Rowe (and our uniquely viral discussion), Joe Polish, and finally Armstrong Williams, not just for having me on your show repeatedly, but also for your groundbreaking *Baltimore Sun* op-ed that confronted America's complicity and caught the US Department of Health and Human Services (HHS)'s attention. You all didn't flinch, and because of that, millions more people now know.

At *The Epoch Times*, this has been a family effort from the start. My wife, Cindy Drukier—we conceived the structure of this book together during those late-night talks, and you always remain my rock of support. I don't know what I'd do without you. Jasper Fakkert, Omid Ghoreishi, and Cindy Gu—your editorial leadership has inspired me and made space for projects like this when few others would. The late Stephen Gregory, who taught me so much about writing and editing—I miss you. Eva Fu—your reporting from the front lines of CCP persecution has been fearless and essential. And to the whole team at *American Thought Leaders* led by Irene Luo, thank you from the bottom of my heart for your exceptional work crafting our episodes exposing China's forced organ harvesting industry, and for doing additional heavy lifting while I was writing this book.

To the editors and commenters who helped shape and sharpen this manuscript: Stephan Zguta, Jon Arlan, Robert Malone, Erik Bethel, Prof. Robert Destro, Roger Garside, David Stilwell, Jennie Sheeks—your insights and dedication to it were critical to realizing its final incarnation. And to my publisher, Tony Lyons, thank you so *very* much for committing so deeply to this book, right out of the gates.

A special thank-you to Prof. Robert Destro (as Assistant Secretary of State for Democracy, Human Rights, and Labor) for his key role in bringing Cheng Pei Ming to America, an act that helped the world finally grasp the full reality of forced organ harvesting.

I owe a special debt to Gordon Chang and Lydia Tam, to Cleo Paskal, and to Heng He, for years of regular discussion and counsel that have profoundly shaped my thinking on the CCP and its strategies.

A particular gratitude to Founder of the Institute of World Politics John Lenczowski for our many thoughtful and patient discussions, through which you imparted to me your uniquely comprehensive understanding of communism.

For further deepening my understanding of the CCP's nature

and strategies—and of the broader ethical battles this atrocity exposes—big thanks to Piero Tozzi, Kyle Bass, Rushan Abbas, Miles Yu, Kay Rubacek, Robert Spalding, Joshua Philipp, Casey Fleming, Erping Zhang, N. S. Lyons, Dean Baxendale, Reggie Littlejohn, Harrison Koehli, Chen Guangcheng, Steven Mosher, Michael Pillsbury, Grant Newsham, Fengsuo Zhou, Terri Marsh, Jim Fanell, Brad Thayer, Anders Corr, Michel Juneau-Katsuya, Nina Shea, Scott McGregor, Curtis Ellis (RIP), Eric Patterson, Levi Browde, Elizabeth Spalding, Christopher Balding, Clyde Prestowitz, Lee Smith, Nury Turkel, Chris Chappel, Yuan Hongbing, Brian Kennedy, Tamuz Itai, Ben Rogers, James Lindsay, and Frank Gaffney. Deep thanks for insights from Rosemary Gibson on medical supply-chain vulnerabilities, Caylan Ford on the Quit-the-CCP movement, Chenggang Xu on your profound work on the uniqueness of communism "with Chinese characteristics" (and Desmond Shum for pointing me towards him), and Wesley Smith on the chilling implications of utilitarian bioethics.

A special thank-you to Dr. Joseph Varon and Ambassador Sam Brownback for their powerful forewords, which brought additional medical, moral, and human rights weight to this book. Ambassador Brownback, your decades-long commitment to religious freedom has been a beacon of hope in this fight. Katrina Lantos Swett, thank you for your own decades of tireless work in this arena, carrying forward the legacy of your father, the late Congressman Tom Lantos, a Holocaust survivor whose lifelong dedication to freedom and human rights continues to inspire me deeply.

To the legislators who have turned evidence into action through championing groundbreaking laws around this issue: Secretary Marco Rubio (as Senator); Senator Ted Cruz; Senator Ron Johnson; Senator Tom Cotton and Senator Chris Coons; Congressman Scott Perry and Congressman Patrick Ryan;

Congressman Chris Smith and Congressman Bill Keating; Congressman Neal Dunn, and to the state legislators who have passed laws related to forced organ harvesting across six states, and counting, your leadership gives real hope that accountability is possible.

I also want to extend deep gratitude to the US Congressional committees and commissions that have kept this issue advancing for nearly two decades. Congressman Dana Rohrabacher, you offered David Kilgour and David Matas the chance to first present China's forced organ harvesting industry to Congress, before the House International Relations Committee's Subcommittee on Oversight and Investigations as far back as September 2006.[1] Congressman Chris Smith and Congressman Jim McGovern, you enacted the Tom Lantos Human Rights Commission's May 2022 hearing, "Forced Organ Harvesting in China: Examining the Evidence," a seminal expose of the facts. Rep. Chris Smith (yes, again!) and Co-chair Sen. Jeff Merkley, you led the Congressional-Executive Commission on China (CECC) to hold the "Stopping the Crime of Organ Harvesting—What More Must Be Done?" hearing in early 2024, and the CECC has included this issue in its annual reports for well over a decade. (A quick note about CECC annual reports: they are dense and packed with facts and required reading for anyone interesting in China human rights).[2] And to the committed people at the U.S. Commission on International Religious Freedom (USCIRF), you have continually stepped up with hearings, reports, and persistent questions, as recently as October 2025.[3] To Chairman John Moolenaar and Ranking Member Raja Krishnamoorthi, your work leading the House Select Committee on the Strategic Competition Between the United States and the Chinese Communist Party (House Committee on the CCP) sets up a path for accountability, with your May 2025 letter to Harvard's president calling out collaborations (some government-funded) with Chinese researchers on organ transplantation studies.[4] It's steps like these that form the beginnings of a movement. I am so grateful to all of you and your work, which played an important role in seeing this book published.

To Master Li Hongzhi, your profound teachings on Truthfulness, Compassion and Forbearance have been a wellspring for me. For the wisdom I've gained, and continue to gain from them, I will forever be grateful. To those millions of Falun Gong practitioners who against all odds have not let your voices be silenced by the CCP, and in so doing have reached multiples of millions, I'm humbled and inspired by your courage, resilience, and sheer grit.

And finally, deep, deep thanks to my parents, who fled communism in Poland in the 1970s, for instilling in me an early awareness of the malign character of that system, and to put me on the road to truly understanding its nature. To my mother, Krystyna, you persevered through many hardships to bring me into the world, and to my brother Rob, you have taken advantage of the modest foundations our parents built from nothing to build further, to truly live the American Dream. In different yet profound ways, you both remind me why we fight!

There are so many others—sources, quiet encouragers, and vocal cheerleaders whose names I can't list here, there just isn't the space. And to those I may have missed, as I've suggested to take stock of the entirely of this work over the last twenty years, if I left you out, please forgive me. You know who you are. You have my deepest gratitude.

Thank you, everyone, for helping me see this book through to the finish.

Jan Jekielek
January 2026

ENDNOTES

Introduction

1 Delaney, Joan. "Whistleblower: ExHusband Forcibly Removed Corneas From 2,000 Living Prisoners." *The Epoch Times*, March 8, 2019; updated June 17, 2019. https://www.theepochtimes.com/china/whistleblower-ex-husband-forcibly-removed-corneas-from-2000-living-prisoners2826955.

2 ChinaTribunal. "Judgment—ChinaTribunal." *China Tribunal*, March 2020. https://chinatribunal.com/final-judgment.

3 "The Rise and Resilience of Falun Gong." *Faluninfo.net*, April 24, 2019. https://faluninfo.net/rise-and-resilience-of-falun-gong.

4 China Tribunal. *China Tribunal Full Judgment—Judgment of The Independent Tribunal into Forced Organ Harvesting from Prisoners of Conscience in China*, March 1, 2020, 151. https://chinatribunal.com/wp-content/uploads/2020/03/ChinaTribunal_JUDGMENT_1stMarch_2020.pdf.

5 *Appendix 1: Investigation Recording of Bai Shuzhong, former health minister of the General Logistics Department of the People's Liberation Army*, PDF, China Tribunal, accessed January 9, 2026, https://chinatribunal.com/wp-content/uploads/2020/02/Appendix-1-Investigation-Recording

-of-Bai-Shuzhong-former-health-minister-of-the-General-Logistics-Department-of-the-People's-Liberation-Army.pdf.

6 Fu, Eva, and Jan Jekielek. "China's 981 Project: Dark Connections Behind the Quest for Longevity." *The Epoch Times*, November 11, 2025; updated December 17, 2025. https://www.theepochtimes.com/article/chinas981projectdarkconnectionsbehindthequestforlongevity5926103.

7 Li, Zhisui. *The Private Life of Chairman Mao: The Memoirs of Mao's Personal Physician.* New York: Random House, 1994.

8 Fu, Eva, and Jan Jekielek. "China's 981 Project: Dark Connections Behind the Quest for Longevity." *The Epoch Times*, November 11, 2025; updated December 17, 2025. https://www.theepochtimes.com/article/chinas-981-project-dark-connections-behind-the-quest-for-longevity-5926103.com.

9 Josh Rudolph, "Translation: Deleted Ad Reveals Death-defying Health Plan for Officials," *China Digital Times*, September 18, 2019, https://chinadigitaltimes.net/2019/09/translation-deleted-ad-reveals-death-defying-health-plan-for-officials/.; 自由亚洲电台 (@RFA_Chinese), "【中共领导人保健以150岁为目标】【301医院广告疑泄密急下架】周日大陆微信疯传一条'981首长健康工程' . . . " X (formerly Twitter), June 27, 2019, *Tweet*, https://x.com/rfa_chinese/status/1173543182811844608.

10 Fu, Eva, and Jan Jekielek. "China's 981 Project: Dark Connections Behind the Quest for Longevity." *The Epoch Times*, November 11, 2025; updated December 17, 2025. https://www.theepochtimes.com/article/chinas-981-project-dark-connections-behind-the-quest-for-longevity-5926103.

Chapter 1

1 Delaney, Joan. "Whistleblower: ExHusband Forcibly Removed Corneas From 2,000 Living Prisoners." *The*

Epoch Times, March 8, 2019; updated June 17, 2019. https://www.theepochtimes.com/china/whistleblower-ex-husband-forcibly-removed-corneas-from-2000-living-prisoners-2826955.

2 Delaney, Joan. "Whistleblower: Ex-Husband Forcibly Removed Corneas from 2,000 Living Prisoners," *The Epoch Times*, March 8, 2019, https://www.theepochtimes.com/china/whistleblower-ex-husband-forcibly-removed-corneas-from-2000-living-prisoners-2826955.

3 Lavee, Jacob, M.D. "State Organs: Independent Tribunal into Forced Organ Harvesting in China—Witness Testimony." *China Tribunal*, March 2019. PDF. https://chinatribunal.com/wp-content/uploads/2019/03/A02_B_State-Organs-Prof-Jacob-Lavee-.pdf.

4 "2008 — Israel Organ Transplantation Law." *The International Coalition to End Transplant Abuse in China*, 2008. https://endtransplantabuse.org/2008israelorgantransplantationlaw.

5 See *Avenues of Escape*, a documentary about this escape route from China, directed by Leon Lee (2017).

6 Johnson, Ian. "A Deadly Exercise: Practicing Falun Gong Was a Right, Ms. Chen Said, to Her Last Day." *The Wall Street Journal*, April 25, 2000. https://www.wsj.com/articles/SB956186343489597132.; Johnson, Ian. "Falun Gong: How One Chinese City Resorted to Atrocities to Control Falun Dafa." *The Wall Street Journal*, (publication date unclear in public archive; circa late 2000). https://www.wsj.com.

7 Jekielek, Jan. "Organ Harvesting in Chinese Death Camps Discussed at Auschwitz Forum." *The Epoch Times*, May 10, 2006; updated August 19, 2019. https://www.theepochtimes.com/china/organ-harvesting-in-chinese-death-camps-discussed-at-auschwitz-forum-2094817.

8 "Hearing Before the 109th Congress" (Document No. 29862). *US Government Publishing Office*, archived March 3, 2016. PDF. https://web.archive.org/web/20160303222135/https://bulk.resource.org/gpo.gov/hearings/109h/29862.pdf.

9 Matas, David and David Kilgour, "Bloody Harvest: Revised Report into Allegations of Organ Harvesting of Falun Gong Practitioners in China," January 31, 2007, https://dafoh.org/matas-kilgour-report.

Chapter 2

1 Jekielek, Jan. "Horrific New Evidence of China Organ Harvesting Revealed." *The Epoch Times*, November 16, 2006; updated July 3, 2015. https://www.theepochtimes.com/article/horrific-new-evidence-of-china-organ-harvesting-revealed-1415685.

2 Jekielek, Jan. "Horrific New Evidence of China Organ Harvesting Revealed," *The Epoch Times*, November 16, 2006, https://www.theepochtimes.com/article/horrific-new-evidence-of-china-organ-harvesting-revealed-1415685.

Chapter 4

1 Jekielek, Jan. "Li Weixun: Rescued from Hell," *The Epoch Times*, June 8, 2007, https://www.theepochtimes.com/article/li-weixun-rescued-from-hell-2170551.

2 Matas, David (response). "ETAC_Question_Chinese Terminology_ReligionORCult." *China Tribunal/ International Coalition to End Transplant Abuse in China*, June 2019. PDF. https://chinatribunal.com/wp-content/uploads/2019/06/ETAC_Question_ChineseTerminology_ReligionORCult.pdf.

3 "Jiang Zemin's Crime of Genocide in the Persecution of Falun Gong." *Uphold Justice*, August 24, 2004. https://www.upholdjustice.org/node/89.

4 "Live: Global Quitting CCP Center Forum on Defending . . . ," YouTube video, 23:39, posted by *Global Service Center for Quitting the CCP*, October 9, 2024, https://www.youtube.com/watch?v=ZTlFOlVVV2k.

(The section referenced seen here: https://x.com/JanJekielek/status/1946002226918359275.)

5 "Flip Flopping in China Over Sourcing Organs from Prisoners." *The International Coalition to End Transplant Abuse in China*, accessed January 7, 2026. https://endtransplantabuse.org/flipfloppinginchinaoversourcingorgansfromprisoners.

6 Gutmann, Ethan. "Bitter Harvest: China's 'Organ Donation' Nightmare," *World Affairs Journal*, July 2012, https://web.archive.org/web/20150323020421/http://www.worldaffairsjournal.org/article/bitter-harvest-china's-'organ-donation'-nightmare.

7 Jekielek, Jan. "How the CCP Dupes the West—and We Keep Falling for It | Chenggang Xu," *EpochTV* (*The Epoch Times*), August 26, 2025, https://www.theepochtimes.com/epochtv/how-the-ccp-dupes-the-west-and-we-keep-falling-for-it-chenggang-xu-5905977.

Chapter 5

1 Pei Ming Cheng, interview by the Center for Human Rights, Catholic University of America, "Forced Organ Harvesting in Communist China: Interview with Pei Ming Cheng (Part 1)," *Center for Human Rights*, https://humanrights.catholic.edu/forced-organ-harvesting-in-communist-china-interview-with-peiming-cheng-part-1.

2 Nazeer, Tasnim. "First Known Survivor of China's Forced Organ Harvesting Speaks Out," *The Diplomat*, August 10,

2024, https://thediplomat.com/2024/08/first-known-survivor-of-chinas-forced-organ-harvesting-speaks-out.

3 Fu, Eva. "Man Who Survived Removal of Part of Liver, Lung in Chinese Prison Speaks Out," *The Epoch Times*, August 9, 2024, updated August 13, 2024, https://www.theepochtimes.com/china/man-who-survived-removal-of-part-of-liver-lung-in-chinese-prison-speaks-out-5703183.

4 Fu, Eva. "Man Who Survived Removal of Part of Liver, Lung in Chinese Prison Speaks Out," *The Epoch Times*, August 9, 2024, updated August 13, 2024, https://www.theepochtimes.com/china/man-who-survived-removal-of-part-of-liver-lung-in-chinese-prison-speaks-out-5703183.

5 "Experts Verify That Falun Gong Practitioner Cheng Peiming Was a Victim of Organ Harvesting." *Minghui.org*, August 15, 2024. https://en.minghui.org/html/articles/2024/8/15/219523.html.

6 Ibid.

7 Fu, Eva. "Man Who Survived Removal of Part of Liver, Lung in Chinese Prison Speaks Out." *Epoch Times*, August 9, 2024. https://www.theepochtimes.com/china/man-who-survived-removal-of-part-of-liver-lung-in-chinese-prison-speaks-out-5703183.

8 Fu, Eva and Jan Jekielek. "CCP Implicates Itself by Attacking Survivor of Forced Organ Harvesting: Human Rights Watchers," *The Epoch Times*, September 10, 2024 (updated August 24, 2025), https://www.theepochtimes.com/china/ccp-implicates-itself-by-attacking-survivor-of-forced-organ-harvesting-human-rights-watchers-5719329.

9 "Organ Procurement and Judicial Execution in China." *Human Rights Watch/Asia*, August 1994. https://www.hrw.org/reports/1994/china1/china_948.htm.

10 Lavee, Jacob, M.D. "Independent Tribunal into Forced Organ Harvesting in China: Witness Testimony—The

Impact of the Use of Organs from Executed Prisoners in China on the New Organ Transplantation Law in Israel." *China Tribunal / Independent Tribunal into Forced Organ Harvesting in China*, March 2019. PDF. https://chinatribunal.com/wp-content/uploads/2019/03/A02_B_State-Organs-Prof-Jacob-Lavee-.pdf.

11 Delaney, Joan. "Whistleblower: ExHusband Forcibly Removed Corneas From 2,000 Living Prisoners." *The Epoch Times*, March 8, 2019; updated June 17, 2019. www.theepochtimes.com/china/whistleblower-ex-husband-forcibly-removed-corneas-from-2000-living-prisoners-2826955.

12 Jekielek, Jan. "Organ Harvesting in Chinese Death Camps Discussed at Auschwitz Forum." *The Epoch Times*, May 10, 2006; updated August 19, 2019. https://www.theepochtimes.com/china/organ-harvesting-in-chinese-death-camps-discussed-at-auschwitz-forum-2094817.

13 "About Bloody Harvest." *Bloody Harvest*. https://bloodyharvest.info/about/.

14 Jekielek, Jan. "Horrific New Evidence of China Organ Harvesting Revealed." *The Epoch Times*, November 16, 2006; updated July 3, 2015. https://www.theepochtimes.com/article/horrific-new-evidence-of-china-organ-harvesting-revealed-1415685.

15 Rose, Daniel Asa. *Larry's Kidney: Being the True Story of How I Found Myself in China With My Black Sheep Cousin and His MailOrder Bride, Skirting the Law to Get Him a Transplant—and Save His Life*. New York: William Morrow & Company, May 12, 2009.

16 Matas, David, and David Kilgour. *Bloody Harvest: The Killing of Falun Gong for Their Organs*. Winnipeg, MB: Seraphim Editions, 2009.

17 Matas, David, and Torsten Trey, eds. *State Organs: Transplant Abuse in China*. Woodstock, Canada: Seraphim Editions, 2012.

18 Gutmann, Ethan. *Slaughter: Mass Killings, Organ Harvesting, and China's Secret Solution to Its Dissident Problem.* Amherst, NY: Prometheus Books, August 12, 2014.

19 Robertson, Matthew. "Investigative Report: A Hospital Built for Murder." *The Epoch Times*, February 4, 2016; updated June 5, 2020. https://www.theepochtimes.com/china/china-hospital-built-for-murder-1958171.

20 "An Update to *Bloody Harvest* and *The Slaughter*." *The International Coalition to End Transplant Abuse in China*, accessed January 7, 2026. https://endtransplantabuse.org/anupdate.

21 "South Korean TV Documentary Confirms Organ Harvesting Still Occurring in China (v4)." *Vimeo*, uploaded by Doctors Against Forced Organ Harvesting (DAFOH), n.d. https://vimeo.com/280284321.

22 "China Organ Harvest Research Center." *China Organ Harvest Research Center*. https://chinaorganharvest.org.

23 "China Tribunal." *China Tribunal.* https://chinatribunal.com.

24 "Final Judgment—China Tribunal." *China Tribunal*, March 2020. https://chinatribunal.com/final-judgment.

25 "The International Coalition to End Transplant Abuse in China (ETAC)." *EndTransplantAbuse.org*. https://endtransplantabuse.org.

26 Robertson, Matthew P. "Organ Procurement and Extrajudicial Execution in China: A Review of the Evidence." *Victims of Communism Memorial Foundation*, March 10, 2020. https://victimsofcommunism.org/publication/china-organ-procurement-report-2020.

27 "Mandates of the Special Rapporteur on Trafficking in Persons et al., Joint Communication AL CHN 5/2021 to the Government of the People's Republic of China (10 June 2021)." *Office of the United Nations High Commissioner for Human Rights (OHCHR)*. PDF. https://spcommreports.ohchr

.org/TMResultsBase/DownLoadPublicCommunicationFile?gId=26382.

28 "China: UN Human Rights Experts Alarmed by 'Organ Harvesting' Allegations." *Office of the United Nations High Commissioner for Human Rights (OHCHR)*, June 14, 2021. https://www.ohchr.org/en/press-releases/2021/06/china-un-human-rights-experts-alarmed-organ-harvesting-allegations.

29 UN Office of the High Commissioner for Human Rights (OHCHR), *"China: UN Human Rights Experts Alarmed by 'Organ Harvesting' Allegations,"* press release, June 14, 2021, United Nations, https://www.ohchr.org/en/press-releases/2021/06/china-un-human-rights-experts-alarmed-organ-harvesting-allegations.

30 International Coalition to End Transplant Abuse in China, "UN Statement on Forced Organ Harvesting in China," *Against Genocide*, July 20, 2021 (originally published June 14, 2021), https://www.against-genocide.org/post/un-special-procedures-experts-release-statement-on-forced-organ-harvesting-in-china.

31 "Do No Harm: Mitigating Human Rights Risks When Interacting with International Medical Institutions & Professionals in Transplantation Medicine." *Global Rights Compliance*. https://globalrightscompliance.com/project/donoharmpolicyguidanceandlegaladvisoryreport/.; "DoNoHarm: *Business & Human Rights in Transplantation Medicine*." *YouTube*, uploaded by End Transplant Abuse, n.d. https://www.youtube.com/watch?v=i12p6Pajccs.

32 Global Rights Compliance. "Legal Advisory Report: Do No Harm—Mitigating Human Rights Risks When Interacting With International Medical Institutions & Professionals in Transplantation Medicine." *Global Rights Compliance*, July 2022. PDF. https://globalrightscompliance.org/wp-content

/uploads/2025/05/legal-advisory-report-do-no-harm-grc-july-2022.pdf

33 Global Rights Compliance. "Policy Guidance: Do No Harm—Mitigating Human Rights Risks When Interacting with International Medical Institutions & Professionals in Transplantation Medicine." *Global Rights Compliance*, April 2022. PDF. https://globalrightscompliance.org/wpcontent/uploads/2025/05/policyguidancedonoharmapril2022.pdf.

34 Doctors Against Forced Organ Harvesting, *Forced Organ Harvesting from Living People in China: Special Report*, April 25, 2024, PDF file, https://dafoh.org/wp-content/uploads/sites/3/2024/04/dafoh-special-report-04252024.pdf.

35 Falun Dafa Information Center, "First Known Survivor of Forced Organ Harvesting Comes Forward," *Faluninfo.net*, September 14, 2024, https://faluninfo.net/first-known-survivor-of-forced-organ-harvesting-comes-forward.

36 Strong, Russell W. "Statement Regarding Liver Forced Organ Harvesting (FOH) Survivor Case," PDF file, August 2024, *International Coalition to End Transplant Abuse in China (ETAC)* / EndTransplantAbuse.org, https://endtransplantabuse.org/wp-content/uploads/2024/08/Prof-Russell-Strong-Statement-regarding-liver-FOH-survivor-case.pdf.; McGiffin, David. "Statement Regarding Lung Forced Organ Harvesting (FOH) Survivor Case," PDF file, August 2024, *International Coalition to End Transplant Abuse in China (ETAC)* / EndTransplantAbuse.org, https://endtransplantabuse.org/wp-content/uploads/2024/08/Prof-David-McGiffin-Statement-regarding-Lung-FOH-survivor-case.pdf.

37 Robertson, Matthew. *Making Repression Pay: The Political Economy of Organ Trafficking in China*, PhD diss., The Australian National University, 2025, ANU Open Research

Repository, https://openresearch-repository.anu.edu.au/items/e668213ac0e64323a1613e20ae741e66.

38 Robertson, Matthew P., Raymond L. Hinde, and Jacob Lavee, "Analysis of Official Deceased Organ Donation Data Casts Doubt on the Credibility of China's Organ Transplant Reform," *BMC Medical Ethics* 20 (2019): 79, https://pubmed.ncbi.nlm.nih.gov/31722695/; "Execution by Organ Procurement: Breaching the Dead Donor Rule in . . . ," American Journal of Transplantation (2022), https://www.amjtransplant.org/article/S16006135(22)082697/fulltext.

39 Gutmann, Ethan. *The Xinjiang Procedure*. Armin Lear Press, 2026.

40 US Commission on International Religious Freedom, *Annual Report 2007* (Washington, DC: US Commission on International Religious Freedom, May 1, 2007), https://www.uscirf.gov/sites/default/files/202104/AnnualReport2007.pdf.

41 US Commission on International Religious Freedom, *"People's Republic of China" (China Chapter)* in *Annual Report 2012* (Washington, DC: US Commission on International Religious Freedom, 2012), https://www.uscirf.gov/sites/default/files/resources/2012ARChapters/china%202012.pdf.

42 Rachel Ritchie, "China Aid Releases 2015 Annual Report on Chinese Government Persecution," *ChinaAid.org*, May 18, 2016, https://chinaaid.org/news/stories-by-issue/advocacy/uscirf-2015-report-notes-rise-in.

43 United States House of Representatives, *H.Res. 281: Expressing Concern Over Persistent and Credible Reports of Systematic, StateSanctioned Organ Harvesting from NonConsenting Prisoners of Conscience in the People's Republic of China*, 113th Cong., 1st sess., introduced June 27, 2013,

Washington, DC: US Government Publishing Office, https://www.congress.gov/bill/113th-congress/house-resolution/281/all-actions.

44 US Congress. House. *Health and Economic Recovery Omnibus Emergency Solutions Act.* H.R. 1540, 119th Congress, 2025. https://www.congress.gov/bill/119th-congress/house-bill/1540.

45 US Congress. House. *Ensuring Access to Quality Child Care Act.* H.R. 1503, 119th Congress, 2025. https://www.congress.gov/bill/119th-congress/house-bill/1503.

46 Fu, Eva and Frank Fang, "More Than 505,000 Sign Petition Urging Countries to Act Against CCP's Forced Organ Harvesting," *The Epoch Times*, December 15, 2025, https://www.theepochtimes.com/china/over-05000-sign-petition-urging-countries-to-act-against-ccps-forced-organ-harvesting-5958451.

47 FOHpetition.org, *Petition to End Forced Organ Harvesting*, accessed January 7, 2026, https://fohpetition.org.

Chapter 6

1 Robertson, Matthew P. *Organ Procurement and Extrajudicial Execution in China: A Review of the Evidence* (SSRN Scholarly Paper, March 10, 2020), 88 pp., Victims of Communism Memorial Foundation & Australian National University, https://ssrn.com/abstract=3598791.

2 World Organization to Investigate the Persecution of Falun Gong (WOIPFG), "WOIPFG's Investigative Report on the Development Model of the CCP's 'Industrial Chain of Forced Organ Harvesting' along the One Belt, One Road Initiative," *Uphold Justice*, June 15, 2025, https://www.upholdjustice.org/node/835?utm.

3 "About DAFOH," Doctors Against Forced Organ Harvesting, https://dafoh.org/about-dafoh/

4 "Investigative Report: From the Live Organ Harvesting of Falun Gong Practitioners to Becoming the Global Leader in Organ Transplants, and Then to the World's Leading Infant Organ Transplant Quantity and Technology," World Organization to Investigate the Persecution of Falun Gong, October 13, 2025, https://www.upholdjustice.org/node/862.

5 Wu, Alex and Eva Fu, "Former Chinese Military Doctor Leaks CCP Plan to Use Taiwanese Troops as Organ Bank," *The Epoch Times*, June 12, 2025, https://www.theepochtimes.com/china/former-chinese-military-doctor-leaks-ccp-plan-to-use-taiwanese-troops-as-organ-bank-5871639.

6 Fu, Eva and Jan Jakielek, "China's '981 Project': Dark Connections Behind the Quest for Longevity," *The Epoch Times*, November 11, 2025, https://www.theepochtimes.com/article/chinas-981-project-dark-connections-behind-the-quest-for-longevity-5926103.

Chapter 7

1 "Michel Juneau-Katsuya: Inside Communist China's Network of Dormant Spies," *EpochTV*, April 14, 2023, https://www.theepochtimes.com/epochtv/michel-juneau-katsuya-inside-communist-chinas-network-of-dormant-spies-5509751.

Chapter 8

1 Paskal, Cleo. *Written testimony before the US–China Economic and Security Review Commission*, March 20, 2025, Foundation for Defense of Democracies, https://www.uscc.gov/sites/default/files/2025-03/Cleo_Paskal_Testimony.pdf.

2 Kirk, Donald. *China Matrix: The Hidden Power Behind the Deadly Trade War*. New York: Hachette Books, 2023.

3 Carpenter, Ted Galen. "George H.W. Bush's Shameful Kowtow to China: A Cautionary Tale," *Cato Institute*, January 2, 2024, https://www.cato.org/commentary/george-hw-bushs-shameful-kowtow-china-cautionary-tale?utm.

4 Pillsbury, Michael. *The Hundred-Year Marathon: China's Secret Strategy to Replace America as the Global Superpower*. New York: Henry Holt and Company, 2015.

5 Corr, Anders. *The Concentration of Power: Institutionalization, Hierarchy & Hegemony*. Toronto: Optimum Publishing International, 2021.

6 Fanell, James E., and Bradley A. Thayer. *Embracing Communist China: America's Greatest Strategic Failure*. New York: War Room Books, 2024.

7 Chang, Gordon G. *The Coming Collapse of China*. New York: Random House, 2001.

8 Jekielek, Jan. "HHS Warns of China Organ Transplants," *The Baltimore Sun*, November 2, 2025, https://www.baltimoresun.com/2025/11/02/hhs-china-organ-transplants.

Chapter 9

1 Newsham, Grant. *When China Attacks: A Warning to America*. Washington, DC: Regnery Publishing, 2023.

2 "Col. Grant Newsham on CCP Chemical Warfare, China's Fishing Militia, and Strategic Weaknesses," *EpochTV*, April 8, 2023, https://www.theepochtimes.com/epochtv/col-grant-newsham-on-ccp-chemical-warfare-chinas-fishing-militia-and-their-greatest-strategic-weakness-5181108.

3 Fanell, James, and Bradley Thayer. "How US Dollars Built China's Military." *EpochTV*. 2025. https://www.theepochtimes.com/epochtv/how-us-dollars-built-chinas-military-james-fanell-and-bradley-thayer-5607504.

4 Lyons, N. S. "The China Convergence." *The Upheaval* (Substack), August 3, 2023. https://theupheaval.substack.com /p/the-china-convergence.

Chapter 10

1 Lenczowski, John. "Conquest Without War: The Threat of Chinese Political Influence Operations," *The Intelligencer: Journal of US Intelligence Studies* 27, no. 2 (Summer–Fall 2022), PDF, 14 pp., Association of Former Intelligence Officers, Falls Church, VA, https://www.afio.com/assets /publications/excerpts/LENCZOWSKI_Conquest _Without_War_Article_AFIO_Intelligencer_Vol27_No2 _SummerFall_2022.pdf.

2 Nazeer, Tasnim. "Leaked CCP Files Expose Global Crackdown on Dissent." *The Diplomat*, February 2025. https://thediplomat.com/2025/02/leaked-ccp-files-expose -global-crackdown-on-dissent/?utm_source=chatgpt.com.

3 Committee to Protect Journalists, "Epoch Times Printer Damaged in Arson Attack in Hong Kong," *Committee to Protect Journalists*, November 22, 2019, https:// cpj.org/2019/11/epoch-times-printer-damaged-in -arson-attack-in-hon.

4 "What the First Known Survivor of China's Forced Organ Harvesting Reveals," *EpochTV*, September 7, 2024, https: //www.theepochtimes.com/epochtv/what-the-first-known -survivor-of-chinas-forced-organ-harvesting-reveals-david -matas-5719889.

Chapter 11

1 US House of Representatives, Select Subcommittee on the Coronavirus Pandemic. 2024. "After Action Review of the COVID-19 Pandemic: The Lessons Learned and a Path Forward." Committee on Oversight and Accountability.

Published December 2, 2024. https://oversight.house.gov/report/after-action-review-of-the-covid-19-pandemic-the-lessons-learned-and-a-path-forward.

2 Neo, Jocelyn. "Unknown Drugs Given to Persecuted Citizens in China to Stop Them from Speaking Out," *The Epoch Times*, August 3, 2022, https://www.theepochtimes.com/china/unknown-drugs-given-to-persecuted-citizens-in-china-to-stop-them-from-speaking-out-4604243.

3 China: Country Policy and Information Note—Falun Gong, UK Home Office, November 2025, https://www.gov.uk/government/publications/china-country-policy-and-information-notes/country-policy-and-information-note-falun-gong-china-november-2025-accessible.

4 National Catholic Reporter. "Vatican Defends Including China in Organ Trafficking Summit." *National Catholic Reporter*, February 15, 2017. https://www.ncronline.org/vatican-defends-including-china-organ-trafficking-summit.

5 Doctors Against Forced Organ Harvesting. Statement cited in Minghui.org. "China's Lack of Transparency a 'Mask of Deception.'" Minghui, February 16, 2017. https://en.minghui.org/html/articles/2017/2/16/162206.html.

6 Holmes, Ryan Connelly, and Dan Sagalyn. "One Doctor's War on Global Organ Trafficking," *PBS News*, May 29, 2017, https://www.pbs.org/newshour/world/one-doctors-war-global-organ-trafficking.

Chapter 12

1 Smith, Lee. "The Thirty Tyrants," *Tablet Magazine*, February 4, 2021, https://www.tabletmag.com/sections/news/articles/the-thirty-tyrants.

2 Smith, Christopher H. "The Broken Promises of China's WTO Accession: Reprioritizing Human Rights." Washington, DC: US House of Representatives Committee on Foreign

Affairs, March 1, 2017. https://www.congress.gov/115/chrg/CHRG-115hhrg24543/CHRG-115hhrg24543.htm.

3 Rice University. "New Twist on Synthesis Technique Developed at Rice Promises Sustainable Manufacturing." *Rice News*, August 16, 2024. https://news.rice.edu/news/2024/new-twist-synthesis-technique-developed-rice-promises-sustainable-manufacturing.

4 Weissert, Will. "China Hid Virus' Severity to Hoard Supplies, Agency Says." The Associated Press, May 3, 2020. Report on a Department of Homeland Security intelligence analysis dated May 1, 2020 (not classified but marked "for official use only"), obtained by The Associated Press.

Chapter 13

1 *Global Service Center for Quitting the Chinese Communist Party*, "Global Tuidang," accessed January 9, 2026, https://global.tuidang.org.

2 "Nine Commentaries on the Communist Party," *The Epoch Times*. New York: Epoch Times/Yih Chyun Corporation, 2004. Originally published as a series of editorials in *The Epoch Times* beginning November 2004.

3 Fox News. "Interview with Vice President J.D. Vance," Fox & Friends, aired April 3, 2025, on Fox News Channel.

4 Wu, Alex. "China Rolls Out Unprecedented Plan to Rescue Ailing Property Sector," *The Epoch Times*, November 20, 2022, https://www.theepochtimes.com/china/china-rolls-out-unprecedented-plan-to-rescue-ailing-property-sector-4868652.

Chapter 14

1 United States Commission on International Religious Freedom. "Freedom Forsaken: Falun Gong and Beijing's Playbook for Repression." USCIRF Annual Report China

Chapter (2025), pdf. https://www.uscirf.gov/sites/default/files/Falun%20Gong--USCIRF%20Testimony%20Freedom%20Forsaken.pdf; US Department of State. 2023 Country Reports on Human Rights Practices: China. Washington, DC: US Department of State, April 22, 2024. (Report condemning forced organ harvesting of Falun Gong practitioners and other abuses). https://www.state.gov/reports/2023-country-reports-on-human-rights-practices.; Congressional-Executive Commission on China. "Hearing Examines the Crime of Forced Organ Harvesting in China." Press release, March 20, 2024. https://www.cecc.gov/media-center/press-releases/hearing-examines-the-crime-of-forced-organ-harvesting-in-china.; Office of the United Nations High Commissioner for Human Rights. "China: UN Human Rights Experts Alarmed by 'Organ Harvesting' Allegations." Press release, June 14, 2021. https://www.ohchr.org/en/press-releases/2021/06/china-un-human-rights-experts-alarmed-organ-harvesting-allegations.

2 Rowe, Mike, host. "438: Jan Jekielek—The Terrible Truth About China." *The Way I Heard It with Mike Rowe*, May 27, 2025. Podcast episode. https://sites.libsyn.com/74011/438-jan-jekielekthe-terrible-truth-about-china.

3 *Is This Really Happening in China? | Jan Jekielek #438 | The Way I Heard It*, YouTube video, 1:24:35, May 27, 2025, posted by Mike Rowe, https://youtu.be/38Dvcz-nhOs.

4 *The Baltimore Sun*, "HHS Issues Urgent Call: Sever US Ties with China's Organ Transplant System amid Ethical Concerns" (opinion by Jan Jekielek), *The Baltimore Sun*, November 2, 2025, https://www.baltimoresun.com/2025/11/02/hhs-china-organ-transplants.

5 US Department of Health and Human Services. "HHS Finds Systemic Disregard for Sanctity of Life in Organ Transplant System." Press release, July 21, 2025. https://

us.pagefreezer.com/en-US/wa/browse/0a7f82bb-be6e-448a-ae11-373d22c37842?url=https:%2F%2Fwww.hhs.gov%2Fpress-room%2Fhrsa-to-reform-organ-transplant-system.html×tamp=2025-12-31T07:02:25Z.

6 Davoli, Joanmarie Ilaria. 2025. "Harvesting Humans." SSRN Paper, January 1, 2025. https://ssrn.com/abstract=5213622. (Removed from SSRN web page.)

7 End Forced Organ Harvesting Rotary Satellite Club, "End Forced Organ Harvesting," accessed January 14, 2026, https://www.efoh.org, and *State Organs: Unmasking Transplant Abuse in China* (documentary film directed by Raymond Zhang, RooYee Films Production Inc., 2024), a documentary exploring allegations of state-sanctioned forced organ harvesting in China.

Epilogue

1 Health Canada. Fifth Annual Report on Medical Assistance in Dying in Canada, 2023. Ottawa, ON: Government of Canada, 2024. Report states that in 2023 4.7 % of all deaths in Canada involved medical assistance in dying, meaning nearly 1 in 20 deaths were MAID.

2 Jauhar, Sandeep, Snehal Patel, and Deane Smith. "Donor Organs Are Too Rare. We Need a New Definition of Death." *The New York Times*, July 30, 2025.

3 Jauhar, Sandeep, Snehal Patel and Deane Smith, "When Are Organ Donors Really Dead?" *The New York Times*, July 30, 2025, https://www.nytimes.com/2025/07/30/opinion/organ-donors-death-definition.html.

4 Abuzeid, Amira. 2025. "HHS Investigation Exposes 'Horrifying' Ethical Failures in Organ Transplant System." *National Catholic Register*, July 23, 2025. https://www.ncregister.com/cna/hhs-investigation-exposes-horrifying-ethical-failures-in-organ-transplant-system.

5 Smith, Wesley J. *Culture of Death: The Age of "Do Harm" Medicine*. Encounter Books, 2016.

Appendix 2

1 End Forced Organ Harvesting Rotary Satellite Club: https://www.efoh.org.
2 https://fohpetition.org.

Acknowledgments

1 U.S. Government Printing Office, *Falun Gong: Organ Harvesting and China's Ongoing War on Human Rights; Hearing before the Subcommittee on Oversight and Investigations of the Committee on International Relations, House of Representatives, One Hundred Ninth Congress, Second Session, September 29, 2006*, Serial No. 109-239 (Washington: U.S. Government Printing Office, 2006), https://www.govinfo.gov/content/pkg/CHRG-109hhrg30146/pdf/CHRG-109hhrg30146.pdf.
2 Congressional-Executive Commission on China, *Annual Reports*, accessed January 14, 2026, https://www.cecc.gov/publications/annual-reports.
3 U.S. Commission on International Religious Freedom, *State-Controlled Religion in China: Hearing Transcript, October 16, 2025*, transcript, McLaughlin Reporting LLC, 2025, accessed January 14, 2026, https://www.uscirf.gov/sites/default/files/Transcript_China%20Hearing%202025.pdf.
4 House Select Committee on the Chinese Communist Party, *Letter to Alan Garber, President, Harvard University, May 19, 2025* (Harvard XPCC letter), accessed January 14, 2026, https://chinaselectcommittee.house.gov/sites/evo-subsites/selectcommitteeontheccp.house.gov/files/evo-media-document/Harvard%20Letter%3AXPCC.pdf.